Oxford English for Cambridge Primary

Workbook

5

Alison Barber
Emma Danihel

OXFORD
UNIVERSITY PRESS

OXFORD
UNIVERSITY PRESS

Great Clarendon Street, Oxford, OX2 6DP, United Kingdom

Oxford University Press is a department of the University of Oxford. It furthers the University's objective of excellence in research, scholarship, and education by publishing worldwide. Oxford is a registered trade mark of Oxford University Press in the UK and in certain other countries

© Oxford University Press 2016

The moral rights of the authors have been asserted

First published in 2016

All rights reserved. No part of this publication may be reproduced, stored in a retrieval system, or transmitted, in any form or by any means, without the prior permission in writing of Oxford University Press, or as expressly permitted by law, by licence or under terms agreed with the appropriate reprographics rights organization. Enquiries concerning reproduction outside the scope of the above should be sent to the Rights Department, Oxford University Press, at the address above.

You must not circulate this work in any other form and you must impose this same condition on any acquirer

British Library Cataloguing in Publication Data
Data available

978-0-19-836633-1

10 9 8 7 6 5 4 3 2

Paper used in the production of this book is a natural, recyclable product made from wood grown in sustainable forests.
The manufacturing process conforms to the environmental regulations of the country of origin.

Printed in Great Britain by Ashford Colour Press Ltd,. Gosport

Acknowledgements
The questions, example answers, marks awarded and/or comments that appear in this book were written by the authors. In examination, the way marks would be awarded to answers like this might be different.

The publishers would like to thank the following for permissions to use their photographs:

Cover: DLILLC/Corbis: p4: Shutterstock; p5: marlenne/Shutterstock; p8: pichayasri/Shutterstock; p9: XonkArts / iStock; p10: Malchev/Shutterstock; p12: Lorelyn Medina / Shutterstock; p14: Glenn Price / Shutterstock; p15: Matthew Cole / Shutterstock; p16: Roslen Mack / Shutterstock; p16: crazzzymouse / Shutterstock; p17: LongQuattro / Shutterstock; p22(t): cherezoff/Shutterstock; p22(b): zebrush/Shutterstock; p33: JorgeAlcay / Shutterstock; p34: James Arrington/iStockphoto; p37: elementals/Shutterstock; p40: Melica/Shutterstock; p42: Shutterstock; p45(t): Tribalium / Shutterstock; p45(b): Cory Thoman / Shutterstock; p46(t): JNT Visual / Shutterstock; p46(b): Doggygraph / Shutterstock; p54: Dannyphoto80/Dreamstime; p55: nuanz/Shutterstock; p57: Julie Ridge/iStockphoto; p58: PILart/Shutterstock; p60: Oleksiy Mark / Shutterstock; p64: upstudio/Shutterstock; p73: Panom/Shutterstock;

Artwork is by: Q2A Media Services Pvt. Ltd, Mike Spoor, Kate Rochester, Chiara Pasqualotto

The author and publisher are grateful for permission to reprint extracts from the following copyright material:

Lillian Allan: 'Anancy' from *If You See the Truth: Poems for Children and Young People* (Verse to Vinyl, 1990), copyright © Lillian Allen 1987, reprinted by permission of the author.

Andy Blackford: 'Tchang and the Pearl Dragon' from *Myths and Legends: Dragon Tales* (ORT Treetops, OUP, 2010), copyright © Andy Blackford 2010, reprinted by permission of Oxford University Press.

John Fardell: extract from *The Flight of the Silver Turtle* (Faber, 2006), copyright © John Fardell 2006, reprinted by permission of the publishers, Faber and Faber Ltd and G P Putnams Sons Books for Young Readers, an imprint of Penguin Young Readers Group, a division of Penguin Random House LLC.

Eleanor Farjeon: 'Bedtime' from *Silver-Sand and Snow* (Michael Joseph, 1951), reprinted by permission of David Higham Associates.

Judith Nicholls: 'Mary Celeste', copyright © Judith Nicholls 1987, from *The Midnight Forest* (Faber, 1987) and 'The Journey', copyright © Judith Nicholls 1990 from *Dragonsfire* (Faber, 1990), reprinted by permission of the author.

Michael Rosen: 'I Left my Shoes by the Door Overnight', copyright © Michael Rosen 2012, reprinted by permission of United Agents on behalf of the author.

Shel Silverstein: 'A Light in the Attic' from *A Light in the Attic* (HarperCollins, 1981), copyright © Shel Silverstein 1974, copyright © 1981, renewed 2002 by Evil Eye Music, LLC; and 'New World' from *Falling Up* (HarperCollins, 1996), copyright © Shel Silverstein 1974, copyright © 1996, renewed 2002 by Evil Eye Music, LLC, reprinted by permission of David Grossman Literary Agency Ltd, and HarperCollins Publishers, USA.

Any third party use of this material, outside of this publication, is prohibited. Interested parties should apply to the copyright holders indicated in each case.

Although we have made every effort to trace and contact all copyright holders before publication this has not been possible in all cases. If notified, the publisher will rectify any errors or omissions at the earliest opportunity.

Links to third party websites are provided by Oxford in good faith and for information only. Oxford disclaims any responsibility for the materials contained in any third party website referenced in this work.

Contents

1. **A world of adventure** — 4
2. **Travels far and wide** — 12
3. **Closer to home** — 20
4. **Tales and legends** — 28
5. **Introduce yourself** — 36
6. **Tell me a poem** — 44
7. **It's a small world** — 52
8. **That's a good point!** — 60
9. **A great performance** — 68

Fiction: Reading *Tchang and the Pearl Dragon* — 76

Word cloud dictionary — 83

New word list — 94

Fiction Speaking and listening • Student book page 8

1 A world of adventures!

My adventure

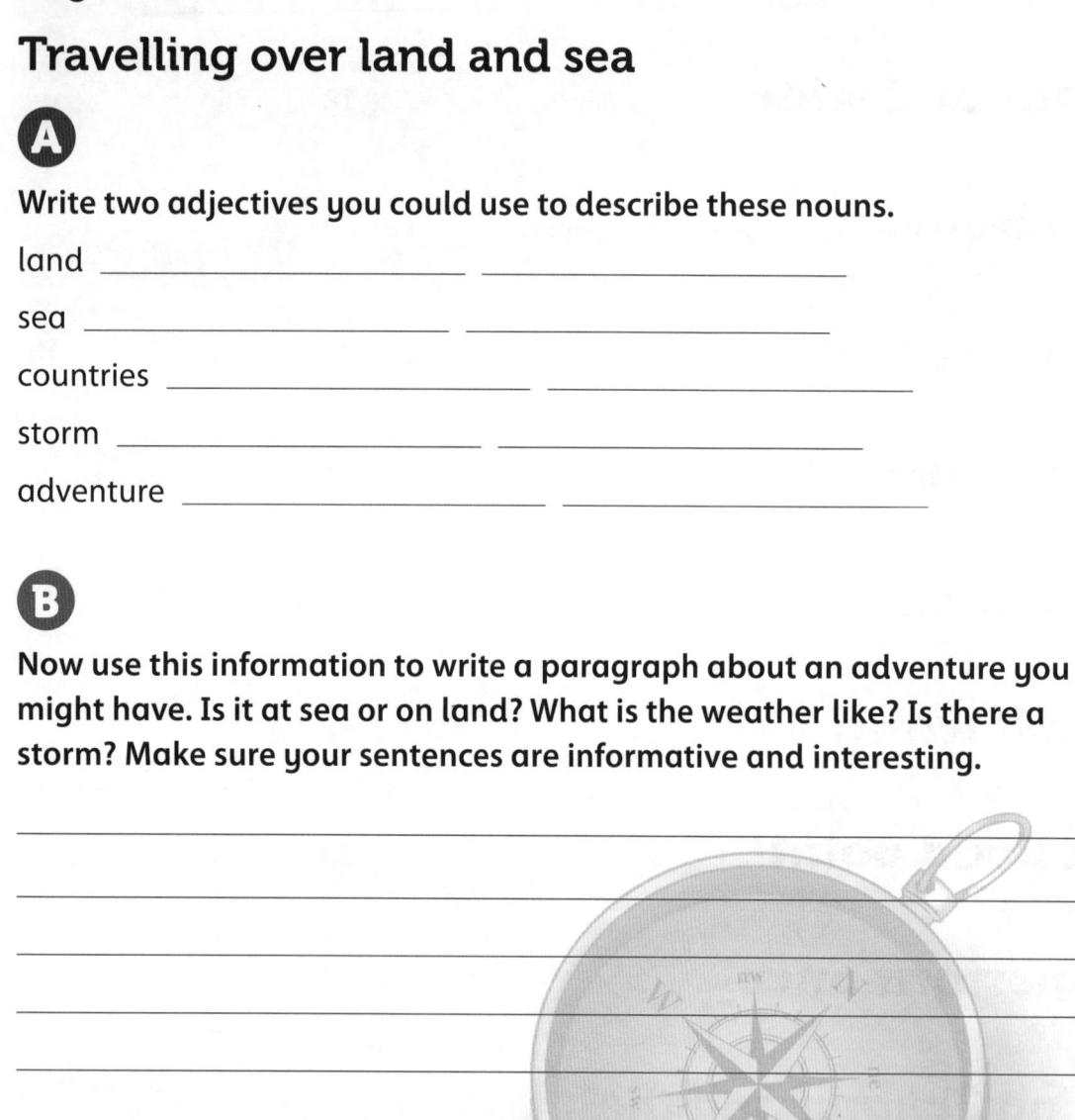

Travelling over land and sea

A

Write two adjectives you could use to describe these nouns.

land _____ _____

sea _____ _____

countries _____ _____

storm _____ _____

adventure _____ _____

B

Now use this information to write a paragraph about an adventure you might have. Is it at sea or on land? What is the weather like? Is there a storm? Make sure your sentences are informative and interesting.

_____
_____
_____
_____
_____
_____
_____
_____

Using metaphor and simile to enrich fiction

The storm

Read the following extract.

Sat in my comfortable, old armchair, sipping hot, sugary tea, and warming my toes by my roaring fire, I could hear the sounds of the ferocious storm, raging all around me like a ravenous lion. My little home, stuck far out on the promontory, shook like a brittle leaf on a gnarled, old tree. The piercing wind whistled down the ancient chimney, rattling the plates on the dresser and bringing an icy chill with it. My time-worn fingers trembled as I bought the sweet, warming brew to my lips and remembered the storm, exactly like this one, thirty years before that had brought the stranger to my door. There had been an unexpected knock. "Who could be out in this tempest, Maggie?" I asked myself. I quickly opened the door and there he was. If only I had known then, what I know now.

A

Write out two examples of similes from the extract.

___

B

Write out two examples of metaphors from the extract.

___

C

How does the writer use similes and metaphors to paint a picture of the extreme weather conditions?

___

Reading for information

The Silver Turtle Takes Off

"Armed police!"
"Armed police! Stand still!"

Before the children could think what they should do, an elderly woman wearing a battered suede jacket came careering round the side of the hangar on a bicycle. "Help me inta* the plane!" she gasped, leaping from her bike and letting it fall onto the pebbles by the slipway. She flung herself at the *Silver Turtle*, her hands grasping the edges of the open cockpit canopy, her feet struggling to find the step-holes in the plane's side. Bewildered, but fearing the old woman might fall backwards, the children held her arms and helped her scramble in. She tumbled down into the pilot's seat, shot out a bony hand, and released the brake lever.

"*No!*" shouted Zara, as the *Silver Turtle rolled* forward. Marcia and Ben both made a grab for the brake lever but, with surprising strength, the woman pushed them back and flicked two switches labelled PORT MOTOR and STARBOARD MOTOR. The propellers whirred into life and the plane hurtled down the slipway towards the sea.

"What are you *doing*?" yelled Ben. He'd got himself back into the co-pilot's seat. Should he pull the woman away from the controls? No – going too fast.

They'd swerve off the slipway and crash onto the pebbles.

Sam clung to the sides of the nose hatch, alarmed and powerless, watching the sea come nearer and nearer…

SPLASH! The plane ploughed into the water and a plume of sea spray cascaded down over the open cockpit and hatch. Without flinching, the woman revved the motors to full speed and zoomed the plane onward through the sea. Keeping one hand on her control column, she punched the undercarriage button and the three wheels whirred and clunked up into the hull.

"STOP!" shouted Zara, sprawled across the back seats with Marcia.

"Stop?" cried the woman. "Are you *mad*?"

PTANG! Something had ricocheted off the plane, just behind the cockpit. Zara looked back through their tail spray and saw two armed men shooting at them from the increasingly distant shore.

The woman was starting to pull back her control column. "NO!" shouted

Sam, realizing what she was doing.

The spray vanished, the sea fell away beneath them and they soared up into the sky. The *Silver Turtle* was airborne.

From *The Flight of the Silver Turtle* by John Fardell

* Scottish people sometimes say "inta", meaning "into".

Comprehension

A

Answer these questions, using the extract to help you.

1 Read the statements about the extract. Which two are true?
   a There are four children in the plane. ☐
   b Ben stops the elderly woman. ☐
   c Armed police fire at the plane. ☐
   d The plane stays on the sea. ☐

2 The writer uses powerful verbs. What effect does this have as you read the extract?
   a They make the story move at a slower pace. ☐
   b They help you to realise it's not real. ☐
   c They suggest lots of quick action and movement. ☐

3 Choose two verbs you think are really powerful and explain why.
   _____
   _____
   _____

B

Read the paragraph starting at line 26 and find **six** past participles that end in *-ed*.

_____   _____
_____   _____
_____   _____

Fiction Grammar • Student book page 14

Making complex and compound sentences

Using 'but' correctly

A

Complete these sentences about yourself.

1 I like _____ and I like _____ in my free time.

2 I like eating _____, but I don't like eating _____.

3 My favourite subject at school is _____, but I don't enjoy _____.

4 At the weekends, I don't like _____, but I really enjoy _____.

B

Choose between 'and' or 'but' to join each pair of clauses.

1 He reads a lot of books _____ he has never been to a library.

2 She fell over _____ hurt her leg.

3 This morning Maria missed the bus _____ she was late for school.

4 Johan asked his friend to come to play _____ he said he was too busy.

5 My sister is very friendly _____ loves meeting people.

6 The boy shouted very loudly _____ no one heard him.

C

Complete these sentences with a suitable ending.

1 I like ice cream, but _____.

2 Tomas works very hard and _____.

3 Tatiana loves her little sister, but _____.

4 Tatiana loves her little sister and _____.

Suffixes

Words ending in –er, –or and –ar

A

Fill the gaps with –or or –er. Use a dictionary to help you.

motivat ____	alligat ____	tut ____	batt ____
activat ____	mast ____	beekeep ____	admir ____
corrid ____	operat ____	adapt ____	tract ____
employ ____	build ____	sail ____	cultivat ____

B

Fill the gaps with –er, –or or –ar to make a noun. You might need to use your dictionary.

creat ____   err ____   teach ____   manag ____   cond ____

ang ____   calend ____   begg ____   sug ____   doct ____

C

Use a dictionary to match the verbs with their definitions. One has been done for you.

motivate — to control or manage something
cultivate — to adjust/change oneself to different conditions
activate — to provide (someone) with a reason for doing something
operate — to raise and grow
adapt — to regard with wonder, pleasure, approval
admire — to make something go

Choose three of the words above and put them into sentences.

1 _____
2 _____
3 _____

Fiction **Vocabulary and spelling** ● Student book pages 19 and 23

Adverbs and suffixes

Adverbs

A

Change these adjectives into adverbs by adding **–ly**. Remember, if the word ends in **y**, you need to change the **y** to an **i**.

angry _____   cheerful _____   funny _____   anxious _____

B

Use the adverbs below to complete the sentences.

tunefully   soundly   neatly
smartly   greedily   heavily

1 The baby sleeps _____.
2 My dad dresses _____.
3 He writes _____.
4 The rain is falling _____.
5 She whistles _____.
6 He ate _____.

Suffixes

C

Choose a word from the list below, adding the **–ful** or **–al** suffix to turn it into an adjective. Some sentences have more than one possibility, so give as many correct sentences for each question as you can think of.

inspiration   delight   colour   power   sensation

1 There was a _____ story about the Prime Minister in the newspaper today.
2 The professor gave an _____ lecture to her students.
3 When he sings he has a _____ voice.
4 The President was a _____ man.
5 The butterfly's wings were very _____.

10 COPYRIGHT OXFORD UNIVERSITY PRESS 2016. PHOTOCOPYING PROHIBITED

Fiction Assessment

Self-assessment on my learning
Unit 1 A world of adventures!

Name _____

Date _____

☺ I understand and can do this well.

😐 I understand but I am not confident.

☹ I don't understand and find this difficult.

Learning objective	☺	😐	☹
Reading skills			
I can identify similes and metaphors.			
Writing skills			
I can use adjectives well to make an adventure story more interesting.			
Language skills			
I understand and can use adverbs well.			
I can combine simple sentences to make compound and complex sentences using the conjunctions 'and' and 'but'.			
I understand the rules for using –er, –or and –ar noun endings.			

I would like more help with _____

_____

_____

_____

2 Travels far and wide

Commas and connectives

Where does the comma go?

A

Put the missing commas into the following sentences. Sometimes more than one comma is missing.

1 As it is your birthday I have decided to take you out.
2 If I had a horse I would call it Silver.
3 Yesterday it was pouring with rain but today it is nice and sunny.
4 I went to see the new film at our local cinema but I didn't enjoy it.
5 As it is sunny today we are going to the beach but not for very long as I have work to do.
6 Alisha's sister the girl who is sitting on the left is getting married in two weeks.

Which connective?

B

Choose the best connectives from the two in brackets to complete the following sentences.

Example: We ate lunch early **because** we were going out. (so/because)

1 He was tired _____ he went to bed early. (so/because)
2 I wasn't surprised _____ he wanted to be a doctor. (that/so)
3 I will need to buy more wood _____ winter will be here soon. (if/because)
4 We will stay at home _____ it rains tomorrow. (if/because)
5 He stood on the box _____ he wanted to see over the fence. (so/because)

Using adverbs

Adverbial phrases

A

Add one of the adverbs in the list to the adverbs in each of the sentences to make an adverbial phrase.

quite   rather   very   surprisingly   extremely

1 My sister spoke to me _____ rudely.
2 "Get out of here," Massoud said _____ menacingly.
3 Carlos felt _____ poorly, so he didn't go to school.
4 Although he did no revision, Anush did _____ brilliantly in his exams.
5 It wasn't her best result, but she was still _____ happy with the result.

B

Add suitable –ly words in the spaces.

George and Erika waited _____ at the side of the stage. Erika checked George's bow-tie was fastened _____ and then they walked _____ onto the stage.

"Ready?" asked George _____.

"Yes." replied Erika _____ .

George played the piano _____ as Erika's voice rang out _____ around the hall. Their parents sat _____ in the audience and clapped _____ at the end of the performance.

C

Make three sentences using adverbs from B.

1 _____

2 _____

3 _____

Fantastic facts about the future

Reading for understanding

A

Read this extract and then answer the questions on page 15.

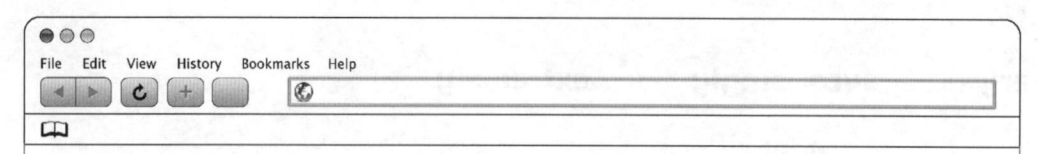

With the recent advancements in technology, human-like robots look set to play an increasingly important role in the lives of humans. They might, in the near future, take the place of company receptionists; care workers to the elderly; home helps; or even become carers to our children.

Research has shown that, far from being distressed by contact with humanoid robots, the young generation sympathise with them and that they personified them with certain of their own attributes.

Young children, between the ages of four and five, were put in a room with a humanoid robot which was secretly being controlled by scientists in another room using remote control. When questioned later, the children believed that the robot had portrayed feelings, that it had shown empathy towards them and that it was capable of being their friend. The children also felt it deserved fair treatment.

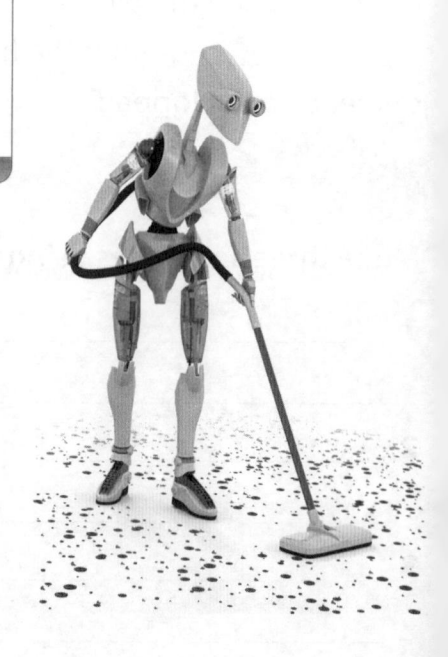

Non-fiction Comprehension • Student book pages 40 and 41

1 Write three of the jobs the article suggests robots might be doing in the future.

_____   _____   _____

2 What kind of relationship did the young children believe they had with the robot?

_____

_____

3 Did the young children like the robot? How do you know?

_____

_____

B

1 Why did the scientists operate the robot by remote control in another room?

_____

_____

2 Why would this experiment not work so well with older children or adults?

_____

_____

3 Would it have made a difference to the experiments if the robot had not been made to look like a human?

_____

_____

C

Replace the underlined words in the text with one of the words or phrases below. Keep the same meaning as the original word.

feel for _____   humanised _____

troubled _____   part _____

shown _____   just _____

warmth _____   features _____

Paragraphs in non-fiction text

Read this report about a festival in Canada.

The Carnival d'Hiver is the largest and most exciting winter festival in the world. It is held every year in Quebec City in Canada and runs from the end of January until the middle of February. It attracts almost 100,000 revellers from all around the world. There are so many thrilling activities for people of all ages, including snow-rafting, dogsled races, skating, sleighing and ice-sculpture contests. Children can even enjoy sliding down from the top of the ice palace! The last night of the Carnival is the most spectacular, as marching bands, clowns, dancers and street performers parade through the streets of Quebec in brightly coloured costumes, entertaining the delighted crowds lining the pavements.

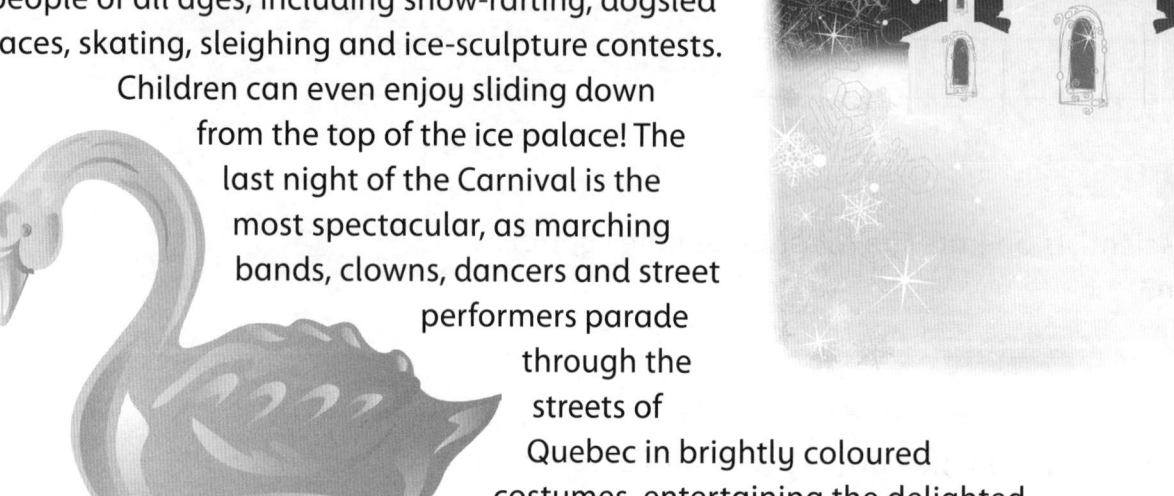

A

Give the report a suitable title and organise the text into three paragraphs. Make a line like this / in the report where each new paragraph should begin.

Give each of the paragraphs a subheading.

Report title: _____

Paragraph title 1: _____

Paragraph title 2: _____

Paragraph title 3: _____

Non-fiction Writing and vocabulary • Student book page 43

B

Write three short paragraphs about a festival or celebration in your country. Include information about the time of year, how long it lasts, who goes and what you can do at it.

1 _____
_____
_____
_____
_____

2 _____
_____
_____
_____
_____

3 _____
_____
_____
_____
_____

C

Look at the three paragraphs you have written about a festival or celebration in your country. Give examples from what you have written to show where you have included the following features of a report.

- written in the present tense _____
- use of a formal style _____
- third person used _____
- specific vocabulary included _____
- factual description included _____
- subheadings included _____
- passive sentences used _____

Non-fiction Vocabulary and spelling • Student book page 39

Building vocabulary

Foreign phrases

Here are some words that come from other languages that are used in the English language. Complete the boxes below. You may need a dictionary.

bon voyage

Original language: _____

Meaning: _____

Used in a sentence: _____

karaoke

Original language: _____

Meaning: _____

Used in a sentence: _____

déjà vu

Original language: _____

Meaning: _____

Used in a sentence: _____

vice versa

Original language: _____

Meaning: _____

Used in a sentence: _____

villa

Original language: _____

Meaning: _____

Used in a sentence: _____

tea

Original language: _____

Meaning: _____

Used in a sentence: _____

potpourri

Original language: _____

Meaning: _____

Used in a sentence: _____

encore

Original language: _____

Meaning: _____

Used in a sentence: _____

Non-fiction Assessment

Self-assessment on my learning

Unit 2 Travels far and wide

Name _____

Date _____

☺ I understand and can do this well.

😐 I understand but I am not confident.

☹ I don't understand and find this difficult.

Learning objective	☺	😐	☹
Reading skills			
I can use words and phrases from a story to answer comprehension questions.			
I can read and evaluate a non-fiction text for organisation.			
Writing skills			
I can use special vocabulary to write on a topic.			
Language skills			
I can begin to use commas to separate clauses within sentences.			
I can investigate clauses within sentences and how they are connected.			

I would like more help with _____

_____

_____

_____

COPYRIGHT OXFORD UNIVERSITY PRESS 2016. PHOTOCOPYING PROHIBITED

3 Closer to home

Poetry

Shel Silverstein was an American cartoonist. He was also a poet, a songwriter, a musician and a writer.

Light in the attic

There's a light on in the attic.
Though the house is dark and shuttered,
I can see a flickerin' flutter,
And I know what it's about.
5 There's a light on in the attic.
I can see it from the outside,
And I know you're on the inside... lookin' out.

Shel Silverstein

New world

Upside-down trees swingin' free,
Busses float and buildings dangle:
Now and then it's nice to see
The world - from a different angle.

Shel Silverstein

Comprehension

A

1 What kind of atmosphere does 'Light in the attic' have? Tick one of the following.
   a Terrifying ☐   b Funny ☐   c Spooky ☐

   Write one line from the poem to support your answer.
   _____

2 What kind of atmosphere does 'New world' have? Tick one of the following.
   a Terrifying ☐   b Funny ☐   c Spooky ☐

   Write one line from the poem to support your answer.
   _____

3 Write what you think is the most important line/lines in each of the poems.
   _____

B

1 Where is the narrator (the person talking) in the first poem?
   _____

2 In the poem 'New world', what does the writer mean when he writes 'Now and then it's nice to see the world - from a different angle'?
   _____

3 Alliteration is when two words close together make the same sound (e.g. grumpy growl). Find two words with alliteration in the first poem.
   _____

C

1 Three things are odd in the second poem. What are they?
   _____

2 Which line rhymes with line 1 in the second poem? Which line rhymes with line 2?
   _____

3 On a separate sheet of paper, make up a four-line poem that includes alliteration. Illustrate your poem when you have finished writing it.

Poetry Reading and comprehension • Student book pages 48 and 49

Word pictures

Shoes by the door

Read the poem then answer the questions.

> I left my shoes by the front door overnight
> And in the morning they were full of draught
> It slid in under the door, but the shoes were waiting
> They drank it down and now it sat in their bellies
> When I poked my toes and soles inside
> My feet felt a silent unseen gulp.
>
> Michael Rosen

A

Connect the word to its correct definition.

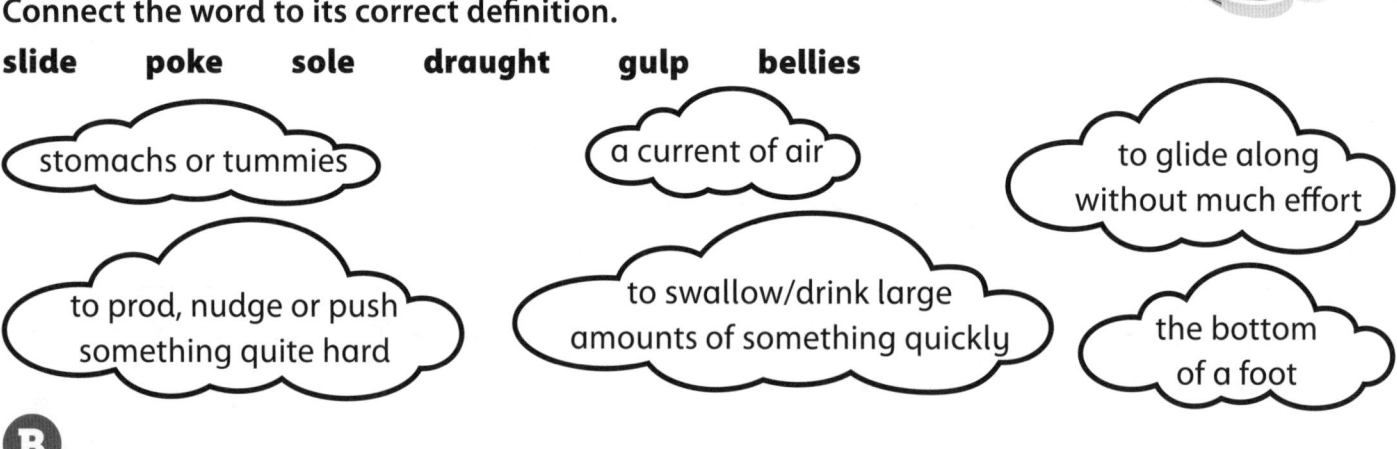

slide   poke   sole   draught   gulp   bellies

- stomachs or tummies
- a current of air
- to glide along without much effort
- to prod, nudge or push something quite hard
- to swallow/drink large amounts of something quickly
- the bottom of a foot

B

Use words and phrases from the poem to support your answers to these questions.

1 Where did the poet leave his shoes? _____

2 Describe in your own words what you think the shoes felt like when the poet put them on in the morning. _____

3 Select words from the poem to support your answer to B2.

C

Find an example of personification in the poem, where an object is doing something that only living things do.

Writing poetry

List poem

It's often easier to write a list poem if you use someone else's beginning and ending.

A

Make a list of things you would like to buy if you went shopping.

B

Fill in the middle of the poem with what you would buy from the shops.

I went to the shops to buy bread
I completely forgot and bought these instead!

I don't think I'll shop again for a while!

Imagery in poetry

Personification

> Poets like to make objects in their poems sound like they are people. *Example:* 'We walked along the sun-kissed sand'. Does this mean that the sun actually kissed the beach? Of course not, because the sun doesn't have lips. However, people do have lips, so this is an example of **personification**.

A

Complete the sentences with a suitable word from the list provided. These verbs are normally associated with human or animal actions. Not all words are used.

> ate   winked   skipped   flew   called
> danced   played   whispered   groaned

1 The tree _____ as it bent over in the wind.
2 The leaves _____ around the playground.
3 The book I was reading was so good that the time _____ by.
4 The tasty box of chocolates _____ to me to eat it.
5 The fast car _____ up the road ahead.

B

Make your own sentences using the remaining four verbs in the list.

1 _____
2 _____
3 _____
4 _____

C

1 Write down what these examples of personification mean.
   a Time flew by because we were having so much fun.
   _____

   b The flowers were crying out for water.
   _____

   c He said he hadn't been jumping in puddles, but his shoes told a different story.
   _____

… Poetry Spelling and vocabulary • Student book page 51

Spelling and vocabulary

Spelled the same but different sound

Sometimes the same letter string has a different sound.

A

Sort these words into the table according to how they sound. The first one has been done for you.

~~flour~~   favour   neighbour   journey   armour   sour   detour
rumour   hour   harbour   journal   court   four   courage   honour
pour   tour   resource

Pronounced as in:		
colour	our	your
	flour	

B

Underline the word that is pronounced differently to the other two.

1 dear   wear   pear
2 niece   field   tried
3 earn   search   year
4 freight   weight   height
5 sought   thought   drought
6 plough   tough   enough

C

On a separate sheet of paper, make a list of:

1 words ending in **ough**. *Example:* though
2 words containing **ear**. *Example:* year
3 words containing **ie**. *Example:* field

Say the different pronunciations out loud and put them in groups according to how they are pronounced.

Writing poetry

Kennings

> A **kenning** is another type of list poem that describes something in clues without saying what it is. Each line has two words, usually a noun and an adjective. A kenning doesn't have to rhyme.

1 Read this kenning. It gives pairs of adjectives followed by nouns that describe the subject on the last line.

2 Now write your own kenning about someone you know. Start by thinking about what they do, look like or sound like. Then change these ideas into two words for each line.

Bubble-blower

Ball-thrower

Drool-dribbler

Paper-ripper

Crayon-eater

Dreadful-sleeper

Toothless-wonder

Kiss-sender

Fussy-taster

Time-waster

Hair-tugger

Mummy-hugger

Baby brother!

Poetry Assessment

Self-assessment on my learning

Unit 3 Closer to home

Name _____

Date _____

☺ I understand and can do this well.

😐 I understand but I am not confident.

☹ I don't understand and find this difficult.

Learning objective	☺	😐	☹
Reading skills			
I can find details in a poem so that I can answer questions.			
I can comment on a writer's use of language.			
Language skills			
I can write my own poem using a list of items.			
I can choose appropriate describing words for a poem.			

I would like more help with _____

_____

_____

4 Tales and legends

A traditional story

Hansel and Gretel

Read this extract adapted from the story of Hansel and Gretel.

Hansel and Gretel were awoken from where they slept, underneath the tree, by the sweet sound of birdcall. Suddenly, a beautiful bird, with feathers as white as snow, swooped down from the sky and landed on a branch just above their heads. It put its head on one side and looked at them for a minute, then flew to a branch further away. The children thought the bird was the loveliest thing that they had ever seen, so they followed it. Each time they almost reached the bird it flew to another branch. On and on the children went, deeper and deeper into the forest, following the little bird.

Then, after a while, they came to a clearing, where there were no trees but a little house instead. The little bird flew over and sat upon the chimney pot.

This was no ordinary house, no ordinary house at all! This house had walls made of divine, golden, velvety gingerbread topped with the sweetest, most delicious, creamy, white icing. This house had windows of scrumptious, clear, melted sugar with gorgeous, delectable red and white striped candy canes as window frames.

A

Answer these questions using words and phrases from the extract.

1 What woke the children up?

2 What did the bird do when it landed on the branch above their heads?

3 Were the children surprised when they saw the house? How do you know?

4 What was around the clear sugar window panes of the house?

Fiction Comprehension • Student book page 61

Finding words in the extract

B

There are eight synonyms (words with similar meanings) in the extract for the words 'nice' or 'nicest'. Find them in the extract and list them below. There are clues for some of them.

scr _____

b _____

sw _____

gor _____

dele _____

_____

_____

_____

Fiction Grammar • Student book page 62

Pronouns

A

The pronouns in the following sentences have been written incorrectly. Write the correct pronoun at the end of the sentence.

1 She gave all her's friends a sweet each. _____

2 My neighbours grow a lot of apple trees in they're garden. _____

3 That pencil is my. _____

4 I don't like going to my cousins' house because there cats are very mean. _____

5 Their house is bigger than our's. _____

6 Tchang's mother had three pearls of his own. _____

B

Complete these sentences by adding a suitable pronoun in the gaps.

1 The children gave _____ books to the teacher at the end of _____ lesson.

2 The group of climbers set _____ the difficult task of climbing the hill at night time.

3 You can give the biscuits to your friends if _____ want _____.

4 My sister and I have short hair but _____ is shorter than _____.

Fiction Grammar and punctuation • Student book page 63

Tchang and the Pearl Dragon
The tale of the missing commas

A

Add the missing commas to this extract from the Tchang story.

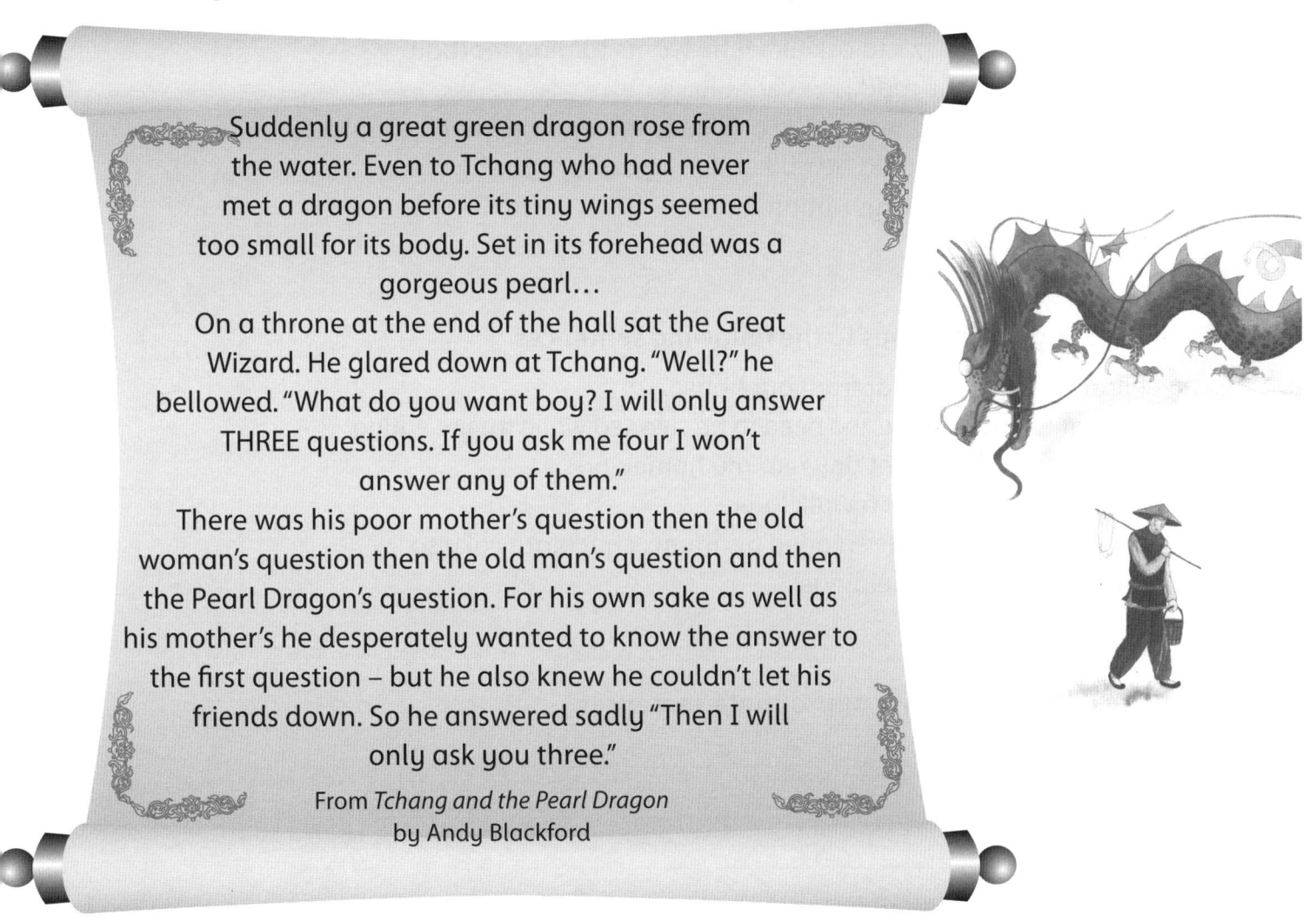

> Suddenly a great green dragon rose from the water. Even to Tchang who had never met a dragon before its tiny wings seemed too small for its body. Set in its forehead was a gorgeous pearl…
>
> On a throne at the end of the hall sat the Great Wizard. He glared down at Tchang. "Well?" he bellowed. "What do you want boy? I will only answer THREE questions. If you ask me four I won't answer any of them."
>
> There was his poor mother's question then the old woman's question then the old man's question and then the Pearl Dragon's question. For his own sake as well as his mother's he desperately wanted to know the answer to the first question – but he also knew he couldn't let his friends down. So he answered sadly "Then I will only ask you three."
>
> From *Tchang and the Pearl Dragon* by Andy Blackford

B

Write out the rule for three of the different uses of commas within the story of Tchang above.

Rule 1 _____

Rule 2 _____

Rule 3 _____

COPYRIGHT OXFORD UNIVERSITY PRESS 2016. PHOTOCOPYING PROHIBITED

Fiction Punctuation • Student book pages 64 and 65

Apostrophes

Possession or shortened form

A

In the following sentences, circle the apostrophes of possession and underline apostrophes showing a shortened form.

1 They're going to Gomez's to ask him if he wants to play football.
2 The girls' school up the road isn't very big.
3 I wasn't looking where I was going and knocked into the man's shoulder.
4 The garage said they would be able to fix my aunty's car by Wednesday.
5 My brother's room is always untidy.

B

Add the missing apostrophes to the following sentences.

1 My childrens school isnt far from our house.
2 All the animals cages in the zoo need to be cleaned while theyre eating.
3 Ill have my dinner then get down to my homework.
4 Its raining so Im going for a walk later.
5 At Khans party all the kids enjoyed his mums chocolate cake so much, they had second helpings!

C

Put the following words into appropriate sentences.

1 bear's _____

2 bees' _____

3 girl's _____

Prepositions

A

Fill in the gaps with a suitable preposition from the list below. You can use each preposition once only, so cross them out as you use them.

up   above   for   about   on   along   at   through   inside   against
in   down   on   across   out   After   into   to   from   off

Leila was walking _____ her road, _____ her way home, thinking _____ the lovely dinner waiting _____ home _____ her, when suddenly she heard a meowing _____ her head. She looked _____ and saw her neighbour's kitten stuck _____ the tree. She tried to call it _____ but it was too afraid. Leila then went _____ the road and knocked _____ her neighbour's door. _____ Leila explained the problem _____ her neighbour, the neighbour came _____ of his house and went _____ his garden _____ a side gate. He took a ladder from _____ his shed and put the ladder _____ the tree. Moments later, the neighbour took the little kitten carefully _____ the tree, and carrying it gently, came _____ the ladder.

B

Write suitable sentences which you can end with the following prepositional phrases.

1 onto the wall

2 through the round window

3 into the swimming pool

4 up the stairs

5 out of the school gates

Fiction Writing • Student book pages 74 and 75

Writing a traditional tale

Getting the opening right

When you are writing a traditional tale or legend, you want to set the scene at the beginning and you want to make your opening sentence exciting so that the reader wants to read on.

Example: Long, long ago there was a lazy hare who was always boasting, to anyone that would listen, that he was the fastest of all creatures.

A

Write two more opening sentences for a traditional tale or legend. You can invent your own story or tell a tale that you know.

_____
_____
_____
_____

Making a plan to write a traditional tale or legend.

You can follow your opening sentence with the following structure:

Problem/action   *Example:* A tortoise challenges the hare to a race.

Resolution   *Example:* The hare is so far in front he decides to have a rest and falls asleep. So the tortoise, who is running at a slow, even pace, wins the race.

Ending/moral   *Example:* Slow and steady is best and don't show off.

B

Write your own plan for a traditional tale or legend.

_____
_____
_____
_____

Self-assessment on my learning

Unit 4 Tales and legends

Name _____

Date _____

☺ I understand and can do this well.

😐 I understand but I am not confident.

☹ I don't understand and find this difficult.

Learning objective	☺	😐	☹
Reading skills			
I can explore the text features of traditional tales and legends.			
Writing skills			
I can write my own legend or fable using typical features of the genre.			
Language skills			
I can use pronouns, making clear to what or whom they refer.			
I can use commas to separate clauses within sentences and clarify meaning in complex sentences.			
I can use apostrophes for both possession and shortened forms.			

I would like more help with _____

_____

_____

Non-fiction Reading and comprehension • Student book pages 78 and 79

5 Introduce yourself

Interviews

Tennis interview

A

Read this interview with the tennis player Danek Hlavacek. Then answer the questions below. JB is the person interviewing Danek.

JB: You were obviously one of the favourites to win, so why have you pulled out of Wimbledon this year?

DH: Unfortunately, it's all down to my back injury. I was suffering from really bad back pain in the French Open and I just haven't fully recovered enough yet. I'm really devastated because I love the atmosphere at Wimbledon – it's the tournament I enjoy playing at the most.

JB: So who is your favourite to win Wimbledon this year?

DH: Well, it is really difficult to say. Nadal and Federer are both great players, of course, but neither has been on good form for the last few months. Ferrer has had a really good year. He's all about speed, but he prefers clay courts to the soft grass courts of Wimbledon. So perhaps this will finally be Murray's year. He's certainly been playing really well recently and he's so eager to succeed at Wimbledon.

1 Why did Hlavacek pull out of Wimbledon? _____
_____

2 Why was Hlavecek unhappy about having to pull out of Wimbledon?
_____
_____

3 Who did Hlavacek think could win Wimbledon? _____

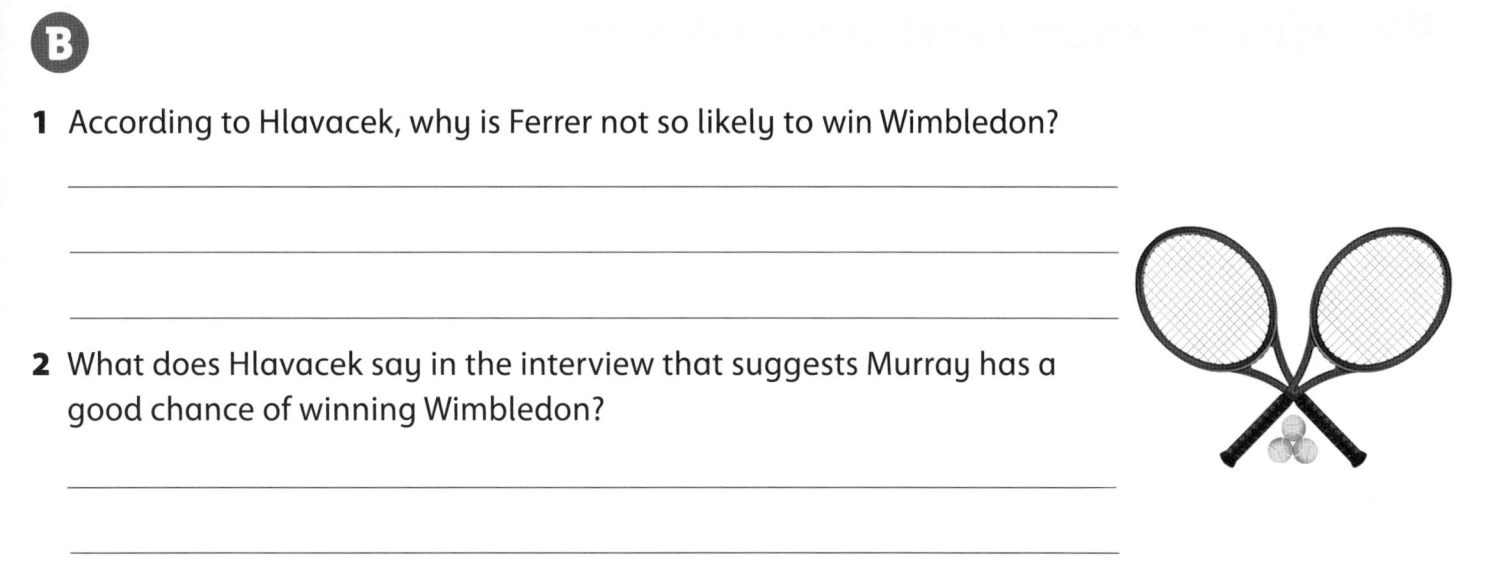

Non-fiction Comprehension, grammar and punctuation • Student book pages 78, 79, 84 and 85

B

1 According to Hlavacek, why is Ferrer not so likely to win Wimbledon?

2 What does Hlavacek say in the interview that suggests Murray has a good chance of winning Wimbledon?

Direct or reported speech

C

Decide which of the sentences below are direct speech and which are reported speech. Ring the correct answer.

1 "Why have you pulled out of Wimbledon?" she asked. Direct/Reported
2 "It's sadly all down to my back," he replied. Direct/Reported
3 He said that it was a problem he had been suffering from at the French Open. Direct/Reported
4 He told JB that it was a shame because he enjoyed playing at Wimbledon the most. Direct/Reported

D

Change JB'S second question in the interview to reported speech.

Non-fiction Writing • Student book pages 82 and 83

Planning your writing project

Writing a biography

A

Name three features of biographies.

1 _____
2 _____
3 _____

B

Plan your own biography of someone that you admire. It could be a sports person, a film star, a politician or a member of your family. Before you write your biography, you should collect information.

Where/when were they born? _____
Where did they go to school or university? _____
Where have they lived and worked? _____
_____
What is their character and reputation? _____
_____
Is there something special that they have achieved? _____
_____
Why do you admire them? _____
_____

C

Write subheadings for each paragraph of your short biography. You can use more or less than four.

Paragraph 1 _____
Paragraph 2 _____
Paragraph 3 _____
Paragraph 4 _____

Non-fiction Grammar and punctuation • Student book page 89

Using commas

A

1 Read this information text from a children's encyclopaedia. You will notice that there are no commas. Insert the commas that have been missed out in the text.

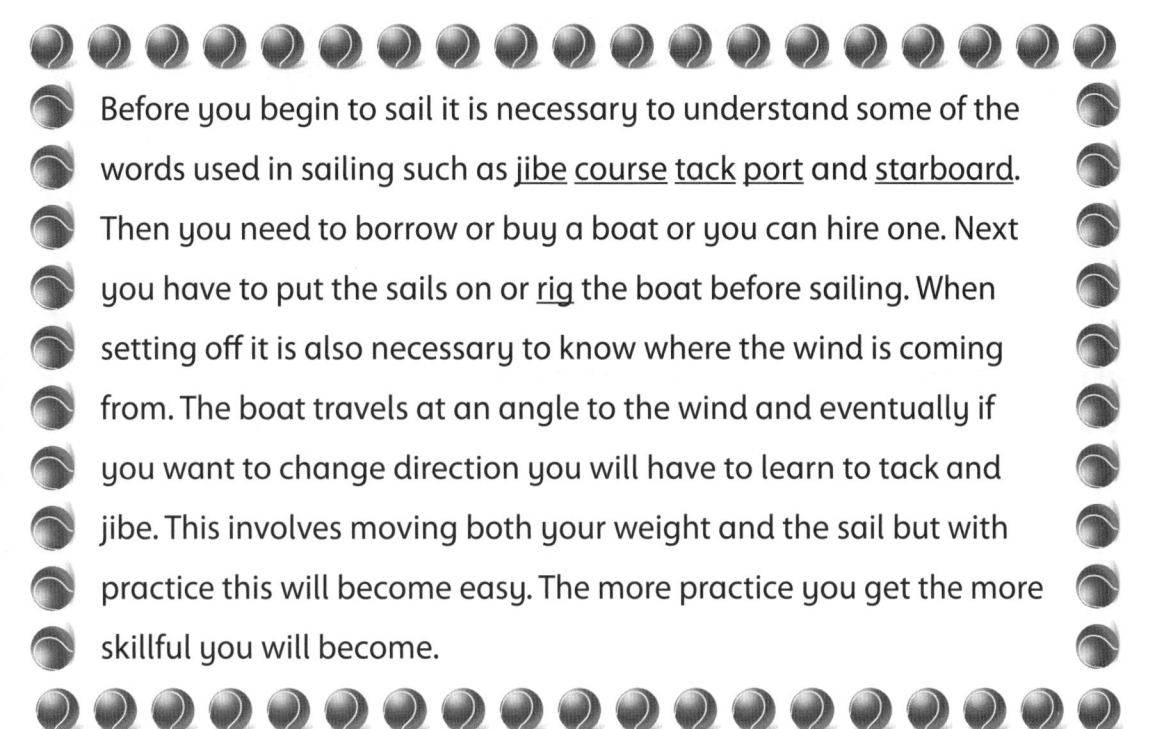

Before you begin to sail it is necessary to understand some of the words used in sailing such as jibe course tack port and starboard. Then you need to borrow or buy a boat or you can hire one. Next you have to put the sails on or rig the boat before sailing. When setting off it is also necessary to know where the wind is coming from. The boat travels at an angle to the wind and eventually if you want to change direction you will have to learn to tack and jibe. This involves moving both your weight and the sail but with practice this will become easy. The more practice you get the more skillful you will become.

2 Draw a line to match the word from the information text about sailing to its correct meaning. Try to work out the correct answer but use the internet or another source if you need to.

jibe	the left-hand side of the boat
course	turning the boat into the wind
tack	the right-hand side of the boat
port	the direction taken by a boat
starboard	change course in a boat by moving the sail

Non-fiction Vocabulary • Student book page 88

Special vocabulary

B

The underlined words in the information text are special vocabulary to do with sailing.

What is your favourite sport? Make a list of special vocabulary which relates to that sport. Use a dictionary or encyclopaedia to help you.

Sport _____

_____   _____   _____

_____   _____   _____

C

Use your list of special vocabulary to write your own information text. You might want to include the following information:

1 How to play the sport _____

_____

_____

_____

2 Where the sport originally came from _____
3 Where it is most popular now _____
4 Important tournaments or competitions _____

_____

_____

5 The best players/competitors of the sport

_____

_____

_____

_____

40   COPYRIGHT OXFORD UNIVERSITY PRESS 2016. PHOTOCOPYING PROHIBITED

Writing genres

Which genre?

A

Look at these opening sentences and choose the genre you think that they belong to.

- autobiography
- news
- information
- diary
- legend
- instructions
- suspense
- biography
- fable

1 Once upon a time, there was a hare who was always showing off about how fast he could run.
   _____

2 Long, long ago, in China, there was a boy called Houyi.
   _____

3 Dear diary,
   We got up late and had Mum's special eggy bread – I love Saturday mornings!
   _____

4 John Taylor was born on 27 May 1947, in a small village called Sawston.
   _____

5 First take four eggs and crack them into a large mixing dish.
   _____

6 As I edged nervously closer and closer to the door, the pitiful, moaning sound behind it became stronger and chilled my heart to ice.
   _____

7 My earliest recollection was the day of my fourth birthday.
   _____

8 The President to announce new measures to combat litter on streets
   _____

9 The Cheetah is a member of the feline or cat family and is found in Asia, Africa and Indonesia.
   _____

Non-fiction Writing • Student book pages 90 and 91

Keeping a diary

Recording what happens

A

Sailor Laura Dekker kept a diary of her solo journey. List three features of diary writing.

1 _____
2 _____
3 _____

B

Write a short diary over the next seven days recording some of the things that happen to you each day. Remember to use informal language.

DAY 1 _____

DAY 2 _____

DAY 3 _____

DAY 4 _____

DAY 5 _____

DAY 6 _____

DAY 7 _____

Non-fiction Assessment

Self-assessment on my learning

Unit 5 Introduce yourself

Name _____

Date _____

☺ I understand and can do this well.

😐 I understand but I am not confident.

☹ I don't understand and find this difficult.

Learning objective	☺	😐	☹
Reading skills			
I can find information in an extract.			
I can explain features of different writing genres.			
Writing skills			
I can write a diary.			
I can map out writing to plan the structure of a biography.			
Language skills			
I understand direct and reported speech.			
I can use special vocabulary.			
I can use commas correctly.			

I would like more help with _____

_____

_____

COPYRIGHT OXFORD UNIVERSITY PRESS 2016. PHOTOCOPYING PROHIBITED

Poetry Vocabulary • Student book page 99

6 Tell me a poem

Vocabulary for poetry
Descriptive language

A

Poetry needs imaginative vocabulary. What you write in poems doesn't have to be true. Write a sentence about each of the following.

Example: The sun is made of tomatoes and orange juice.

1 The sun

2 The moon

3 The stars

4 The clouds

5 The sea

B

Make your sentences into a short poem.

Similes and metaphors

A

Choose the best adjective to complete the following similes.

light   slippery   old   hard   free   white

as _____ as snow   as _____ as a rock

as _____ as a feather   as _____ as the hills

as _____ as an eel   as _____ as the wind

B

Choose the most suitable noun to complete these similes.

an angel   a bomb   cats and dogs   a log

1 The room looked like _____ had hit it.

2 She sang like _____.

3 The two brothers fight like _____.

4 Last night, I slept like _____.

C

Now choose the best nouns to complete the metaphors below.

dream   lion   maze   blanket

1 She has the heart of a _____.

2 Life is a _____ which everyone has to find their way around.

3 I'm so happy, my life is a _____.

4 A _____ of snow covered our village.

Poetry Vocabulary • Student book page 102

More descriptive words

Matching words

A

The nouns, verbs and adjectives below could be used to describe fire, wind, leaves or old people. Sort the words into the boxes. Some words could go into more than one box.

autumn	cyclone	roaring	advanced	green	yellow
red	piercing	inferno	flickering	gnarled	ancient
draught	whistling	burning	pensioner	time-worn	blazing
falling	smoky	crunching	puff	rattling	icy
wrinkly	blowing	brittle	wise	crackling	breezy
chilly	tempest	golden-brown	retirement		

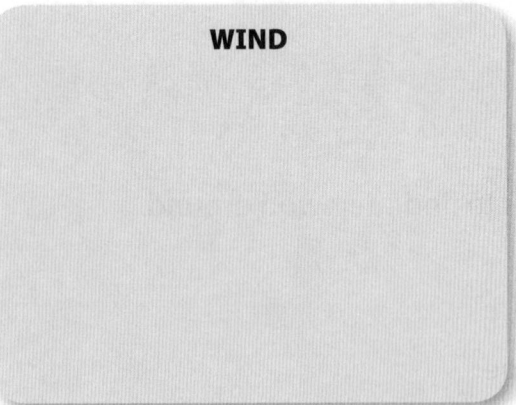

FIRE

LEAVES

WIND

OLD PEOPLE

Poetry Vocabulary • Student book page 102

B

Using the words on the opposite page to help you, write four short paragraphs describing wind, fire, old people and leaves.

1 Wind _____
_____
_____

2 Fire _____
_____
_____

3 Old people _____
_____
_____

4 Leaves _____
_____
_____

C

Below are some words that could be used to describe the sea. Use a dictionary to match them with their definitions.

surf	a sudden forward movement by a natural force like the tide
spray	shine with soft, slightly wavering light
roaring	the line of foam formed by waves
surging	making a loud, deep, long sound
shimmer	liquid that is blown through the air to form tiny droplets

COPYRIGHT OXFORD UNIVERSITY PRESS 2016. PHOTOCOPYING PROHIBITED

Poetry Reading • Student book pages 104 and 105

Narrative poetry

The mystery of the disappearance of the ship called the *Mary Celeste* is a true story. The ship was found out at sea with no one on board. No one knows what really happened, but Judith Nicholls wrote a poem about it using real facts and some made up ideas. Here is an extract from it.

Mary Celeste

Only the wind sings
in the riggings,
the hull creaks a lullaby;
a sail lifts gently
5   like a message
pinned to a vacant sky.
The wheel turns
over bare decks,
shirts flap on a line;
10 only the song of the lapping waves
beats steady time…

First mate,
off-duty from
the long dawn watch, begins
15 a letter to his wife, daydreams
of home.

The Captain's wife is late;
the child did not sleep
the breakfast has passed…
20 She, too, is missing home;
sits down at last to eat,
but can't quite force
the porridge down.
She swallows hard,
25 slices the top from her egg.

The second mate
is happy.
A four hour sleep,
full stomach
and a quiet sea   30
are all he craves.
He has all three.

Judith Nicholls

Glossary
craves needs something badly
first mate second in command on a ship
lullaby a quiet song sung to children to send them to sleep
riggings ropes that support the mast of a ship
porridge a breakfast of oats and hot milk or water
second mate third in command on a ship

Poetry Writing • Student book pages 104 and 105

A

The first verse describes the empty ship. The second verse describes the first mate. Then the poem goes on to describe the Captain's wife and the second mate.

How are the Captain's wife, the first mate and the second mate described in the poem?

1 The Captain's wife

_____

_____

2 The first mate

_____

_____

3 The second mate

_____

_____

B

Write a summary of the extract below **in 40 words or less.**

There are a few facts that are known about the *Mary Celeste*. There had been ten people on board the doomed ship, including the Captain, his wife and their baby daughter. It is also known that an entry was made in the ship's log book on 25 November, the very last one made by the crew, and that there had been a storm later that day. The ship was found drifting at sea ten days later, completely undamaged. However, there was no sign of the Captain, his family, or the rest of the crew. The ship's boats were gone but most other things, including personal belongings, were left behind.

C

There are many theories about what happened to the crew of the *Mary Celeste*. Research the story and decide on your own explanation. Write your ideas here.

_____

_____

_____

COPYRIGHT OXFORD UNIVERSITY PRESS 2016. PHOTOCOPYING PROHIBITED

Poetry Writing • Student book pages 104 and 105

Writing a narrative poem

Telling a story

A narrative poem needs to set the scene at the beginning, just like a story, with a character. Then it needs a plot, action and an ending.

The Journey
I am the acorn
that grew the oak
that gave the plank the Vikings took
to make the boat
to sail them out
across the seas
to England.

Judith Nichols

A

1 Describe the scene at the start of the poem.
_____

2 What is the action in the poem?
_____

3 What happened at the end?
_____

B

1 Why do you think the third line is longer than all the other lines? The poet has achieved something unusual by setting the poem out in this way. If you can see it, explain the effect in your own words.
_____

2 Write your own journey poem about a drop of water.
_____
_____
_____
_____
_____

Poetry Assessment

Self-assessment on my learning

Unit 6 Tell me a poem

Name _____

Date _____

🙂 I understand and can do this well.

😐 I understand but I am not confident.

🙁 I don't understand and find this difficult.

Learning objective	🙂	😐	🙁
Reading skills			
I can read and evaluate poems for organisation and pattern.			
Writing skills			
I can understand and use special vocabulary to write for a specific purpose.			
Language skills			
I understand and can discuss similes, metaphors and personification.			
I can identify and choose appropriate words and sound patterns that are used to create an effect in a poem.			

I would like more help with _____
_____
_____

7 It's a small world

Prepositions

Choosing the correct prepositions

A

Complete the following paragraph by adding a preposition from the list below.

with   towards   in   from   of   At   by   From   by   for   in

Muhammad enjoyed going to school _____ his local village _____ Bangladesh because he wanted to become a doctor and get away _____ small town life _____ getting a good education, _____ excellent qualifications which were suitable _____ getting a place at university to study medicine. _____ these humble beginnings, Muhammad studied hard and advanced _____ his goal _____ qualifying to be a doctor. _____ the end of his training, what do you think he did? Yes, he returned to his home village and thanked his teachers, friends and family _____ becoming the village doctor.

B

Write a sentence for each of these prepositions.

against   between   beyond

1 _____

2 _____

3 _____

Fiction Grammar and punctuation • Student book page 113

Complex sentences

Using a comma to separate clauses

A

Rewrite the sentences below to include the information in the brackets. Remember to include all the correct punctuation.

1 Muhammad went to school in his local village. (which he enjoyed very much)
_____
_____

2 He wanted to get a good education to escape small town life. (with excellent qualifications)
_____
_____

3 Mohammad worked hard and qualified as a doctor. (as he had done at school)
_____
_____

4 Muhammed returned to his home village to be the local doctor. (from which he had previously wanted to get away) _____
_____
_____

B

Add the missing commas to the following sentences.

1 Yesterday I went for a nice long walk along the canal.
2 My best friend who is a year older than me is going to a different school next year.
3 In the end we decided to go home early.
4 By this time tomorrow I will be on a train to Paris which is where my cousin lives.

C

Finish these sentences in your own words. Don't forget to add the correct punctuation.

1 Since last year _____

2 _____ instead of my best friend.

3 _____ next to the sea.

Verbs

Get the verb right

A

Add 'was' or 'were' to complete the following sentences.

1 We _____ on our way home when we met Katarina and Maria.
2 They _____ going to the swimming pool.
3 The cinema _____ showing our favourite film.
4 The children _____ playing in the park.
5 Mum _____ cross because we _____ late home.

B

Complete the sentences by putting the verbs in brackets into the correct tenses.

1 She _____ (drive) to the shops when her car _____. (break down)
2 I _____ (run) to school this morning because I _____ (be) late.
3 Mariam's brother _____ (be) three years older than her sister.
4 We _____ (eat) our lunch before we went to the park.
5 Dom _____ (feel) sick when I _____ (call) him this morning, so we are not _____ (go) out.

Fiction Grammar • Student book page 116

C

Change these sentences from the present to the past, or the past to the present.

1 Anya gets up at 6 o'clock every morning and eats her breakfast before walking to school.

_____

_____

2 I was running late so I was eating very quickly.

_____

3 Complete this extract by putting the verbs in brackets into the correct form.

Tania suddenly _____ (open) her eyes and _____ (sit) up in her bed. There _____ (be) the noise again. She definitely _____ (hear) something this time. She _____ (be) sure the noise _____ (come) from the other bedrooms. Nervously, she _____ (drag) herself from her nice warm bed and _____ (creep) noiselessly to her bedroom door. She _____ (decide) not to turn on the lights but instead slowly and silently she _____ (open) the door. Then, she _____ (see) her younger brother _____ (shuffle) towards the kitchen to _____ (get) a midnight snack!

Fiction Vocabulary • Student book page 117

Synonyms for powerful stories

A 1 Match a synonym from the list below to the correct word in the box.

| sultry | chilly | devour | nibble | furious | radiant |
| grin | merry | dim | blubber | sneak | cranky |

cold	creep	cry
dull	bright	irritable
happy	smile	bite
angry	hot	gobble

2 Write a synonym for each of the underlined words in the following sentences.
   1 The sudden noise <u>startled</u> the children. _____
   2 "I don't want to go for a walk," my sister <u>moaned</u>. _____
   3 The plane <u>rolled</u> down the runway. _____
   4 May was very <u>agitated</u> when she heard the news. _____
   5 He <u>grabbed</u> my hand to save me from slipping. _____

B 1 In the story extract about Tania on page 55, find synonyms that mean 'to walk quietly'.

_____
_____

Fiction Grammar • Student book page 117

2 Think of one synonym for each of the words below then write one sentence using each synonym.

1 bright _____

_____

_____

2 huge _____

_____

_____

3 strangely _____

_____

_____

C

Replace the underlined words in the passage with synonyms which are stronger and more descriptive.

"What's that?" said Sara. _____

"What's what?" said Anika. _____

"That!" said Sara. _____

"Oh, I don't know. It's nothing," said Anika. "Go back to sleep." _____

"I definitely saw something move outside the tent," said Sara. _____

"What's that unpleasant sound?" said Sara. _____

"I don't know," said Anika beginning to feel unhappy. _____

"It's coming closer," said Sara. _____

"I know," said Anika feeling very unhappy. _____

The girls were both scared. _____

"Surprise!" said Mario, Sara's little brother, poking his head through the tent mischievously.

Spelling word endings

Word endings

A Remember the rules for spelling words ending –*ed* and –*ing*. Complete the table below.

comply	complied	complying
flip	flipped	flipping
wade	waded	wading
fake	_____	_____
_____	gripped	_____
_____	_____	trimming
_____	tamed	_____
supply	_____	_____
mop	_____	_____
snore	_____	_____

B Fill in the gaps of the following sentences with a suitable verb ending in –*ed* or –*ing*.

We _____ slowly in our hot air balloon over the top of the forest, closer and closer towards the clearing. It was _____ dark and cold and my heart was _____ so fast I was _____ that I would faint. We were dangerously close to _____ into the trees below us. "There it is," _____ Alberto. We _____ at each other and _____.

"Quick, get the ropes ready," Alberto _____.

"OK!" I _____. But just as we got close to the landing spot the balloon jolted and we _____.

Fiction Assessment

Self-assessment on my learning

Unit 7 It's a small world

Name _____

Date _____

☺ I understand and can do this well.

😐 I understand but I am not confident.

☹ I don't understand and find this difficult.

Learning objective	☺	😐	☹
Language skills			
I understand and can change the tense of sentences.			
I understand and can use a range of synonyms.			
I can spell words using –ed and –ing.			
I can identify prepositions and know how to use them.			
I can use commas to separate clauses and to make meanings clearer in compound sentences.			

I would like more help with _____

_____

_____

Non-fiction Spelling and vocabulary • Student book page 130

8 That's a good point!

Creating opposites, making comparisons

Prefixes for opposites

A

The prefixes *un-*, *dis-*, *in-*, *il-* and *ir-* all mean 'not' and are used to create the opposite meaning of a word. Choose the right prefix to connect to the words below to make the opposite meaning.

dis   un   in   il   ir

_____ happy	_____ trust	_____ like	_____ legal
_____ beatable	_____ even	_____ deserved	_____ content
_____ relevant	_____ equal	_____ well	_____ obey
_____ obedient	_____ logical	_____ dress	_____ popular
_____ zip	_____ please	_____ likely	_____ pleasant

Forming the comparative and superlative

Read the lists of comparatives and superlatives.

adjective	comparative	superlative
big	bigger	biggest
bright	brighter	brightest
white	whiter	whitest
angry	angrier	angriest
careful	more careful	most careful
confident	more confident	most confident

Non-fiction Spelling and vocabulary • Student book page 130

B

Using the examples opposite to help you, write the spelling rules for forming the following comparative and superlative forms.

1 A one-syllable adjective

Example: 'bright': add '-er' or '-est' to the end of the word.

2 A one-syllable adjective ending in 'e'

_____

3 A one-syllable adjective ending with a single consonant with a single vowel before it

_____

4 A two-syllable adjective

_____

5 A two-syllable adjective ending with 'y'

_____

6 Adjectives with three or more syllables

_____

C

Write six more adjectives to give an example of each of the above rules.

1 _____   2 _____   3 _____

4 _____   5 _____   6 _____

D

The following adjectives are irregular and do not follow the rules. Complete the comparative and superlative forms in the spaces provided.

adjective	comparative	superlative
good		
bad		
far		
many		

Non-fiction Spelling and vocabulary • Student book page 131

Sounds the same but different meaning

They're, their or there

A

Fill in the gaps with 'they're', 'their' or 'there'.

1 As my neighbours were on holiday, I watered _____ garden for them.
2 _____ was a huge thunderstorm in the night.
3 I looked in his bedroom, but John wasn't _____
4 We are going to Eshe and Haji's house tonight as _____ cooking us a special dinner.
5 The children looked everywhere for _____ ball but they couldn't find it anywhere.
6 My friend's family are on _____ holiday in Greece and _____ having a great time _____!

Where, we're, wear or were

B

Fill in the gaps with 'where', 'we're', 'wear' or 'were'.

1 _____ did you say you _____ going tomorrow night?
2 We _____ going to the cinema, but now _____ going to the theatre instead.
3 What are you going to _____ to the theatre?
4 I want to _____ my long black dress, but I don't know _____ it is.
5 _____ you happy when you found out your parents _____ taking you on holiday?

Idioms

Everyday sayings

A

Rewrite these sentences using one of the idioms below.

1 They found a solution *right at the last minute*. _____
2 All the noise next door is *making me so cross*. _____
3 We go out to dinner together about *once a year*. _____
4 It was raining *really heavily* all the time while we were camping. _____
5 My father reversed into the garden wall and had to pay *a lot of money* to get the car fixed. _____
6 My English homework was *really easy*. _____

at the eleventh hour   **an arm and a leg**   **once in a blue moon**
driving me up the wall   **cats and dogs**   **a piece of cake**

B

Use one of the words below to complete the following idioms and then match each of the idioms with their correct definition.

hit   thick   hat   teeth   dumps   weather

Idiom	Definition
1 by the skin of one's _____	to leave
2 at the drop of a _____	feeling sick or unwell
3 under the _____	narrowly or barely
4 down in the _____	through both good and bad times
5 to _____ the road	instantly, without hesitation
6 through _____ and thin	miserable, unhappy

Non-fiction Writing • Student book pages 136 and 137

Persuasive language in adverts

A perfect holiday

Advertisements are a type of persuasive writing. They appeal to your feelings by using strong descriptive words. Read this newspaper advert.

European Holiday

Nothing can possibly compare with the wonderful elegance of a fantastic holiday in Europe. Discover amazing and delightful destinations brimming with cultural and scenic splendour. Make 2017 the year that you cruise the sublime Scottish shores, relax on the tranquil, glorious shores of the Italian lakes or experience the breathtakingly spectacular mountain range of the Swiss Alps. Whatever you decide, you're certain to find your perfect European getaway so do not hesitate, do not miss out on this once-in-a-lifetime trip, book now to save disappointment later.

A

Circle all the strong words used in the advertisement, then find their synonyms in a thesaurus or dictionary.
Example: sublime – synonyms: glorious, splendorous, superb

B

Fill in the gaps in this advertisement with suitable strong and persuasive words.

Join us for an _____ journey to _____ (fill in the name of your country here) full of _____ highlights. This will surely be a _____ holiday. You will see _____ scenery and some of the most _____ cities of the world. Our hotels offer the most _____ accommodation at _____ prices. Truly, this will be a _____ experience for you.

C

On a separate piece of paper, write your own advertisement using suitable language to persuade people to come on holiday to a place or area in your country.

Persuasive writing

Writing a persuasive letter

A

Head teacher Mrs Smith has decided to get rid of the lunch break at your school. This means that, not only will you not get any food at lunch time, you will have lessons instead. Max has written this letter to her to complain, but it's not correct for the task. Make notes at the side of the letter to identify what he has done wrong.

Dear Mrs Smith

Eating food is really good for you as it helps people to think better and this will mean that everyone will be able to work harder. I know that teachers want all the children at school to do well and they will be able to study for longer if they don't stop for lunch.

I am writing to you because you have banned lunch break. This will not help our education. I don't agree with your decision and I have decided that I would like to have our lunch breaks back. I demand this!!!!!

Secondly, it might mean that children could suffer from diseases in their later life. We need to go outside to get exercise and fresh air, and we should also have some sort of snack like an apple. It would be good if we could eat this during the lessons we will be having at lunch time.

At lunch break children can socialise and play with their friends. Children will not do better in lessons without fresh air.

Thanks a lot,
Max

Non-fiction Writing • Student's book pages 142 and 143

B
Give five examples of features of persuasive letters that Max didn't include. *Example:* rhetorical questions

Feature 1 _____

Feature 2 _____

Feature 3 _____

Feature 4 _____

Feature 5 _____

C
Rewrite the letter, making it more suitable for persuading Mrs Smith to keep lunch breaks.

_____
_____
_____
_____
_____
_____
_____
_____
_____
_____
_____
_____
_____
_____
_____
_____
_____
_____

Non-fiction Assessment

Self-assessment on my learning
Unit 8 That's a good point!

Name _____

Date _____

☺ I understand and can do this well.

😐 I understand but I am not confident.

☹ I don't understand and find this difficult.

Learning objective	☺	😐	☹
Writing skills			
I can organise and write a newspaper advertisement using persuasive language.			
I can organise and write a letter using persuasive language.			
Language skills			
I can investigate ways of creating opposites and comparatives.			
I can identify different grammatical homophones.			
I can identify and use a number of idiomatic phrases.			

I would like more help with _____

_____

_____

_____

9 A great performance

Performance poetry

Performing a poem

Read this poem and then answer the questions below.

Bedtime

Five minutes, five minutes more, please!
Let me stay five minutes more!
Can't I just finish the castle
I'm building here on the floor?
5 Can't I just finish the story
I'm reading here in my book?
Can't I just finish this bead-chain --
It *almost* is finished, look!
Can't I just finish this game, please?
10 When a game's once begun
It's a pity never to find out
Whether you've lost or won.
Can't I just stay five minutes?
Well, can't I just stay just four?
15 Three minutes, then? two minutes?
Can't I stay *one* minute more?

Eleanor Farjeon

A

1 What four things does the child want to stay up and do?

_____ _____

_____ _____

2 What one thing has the child nearly finished?

_____

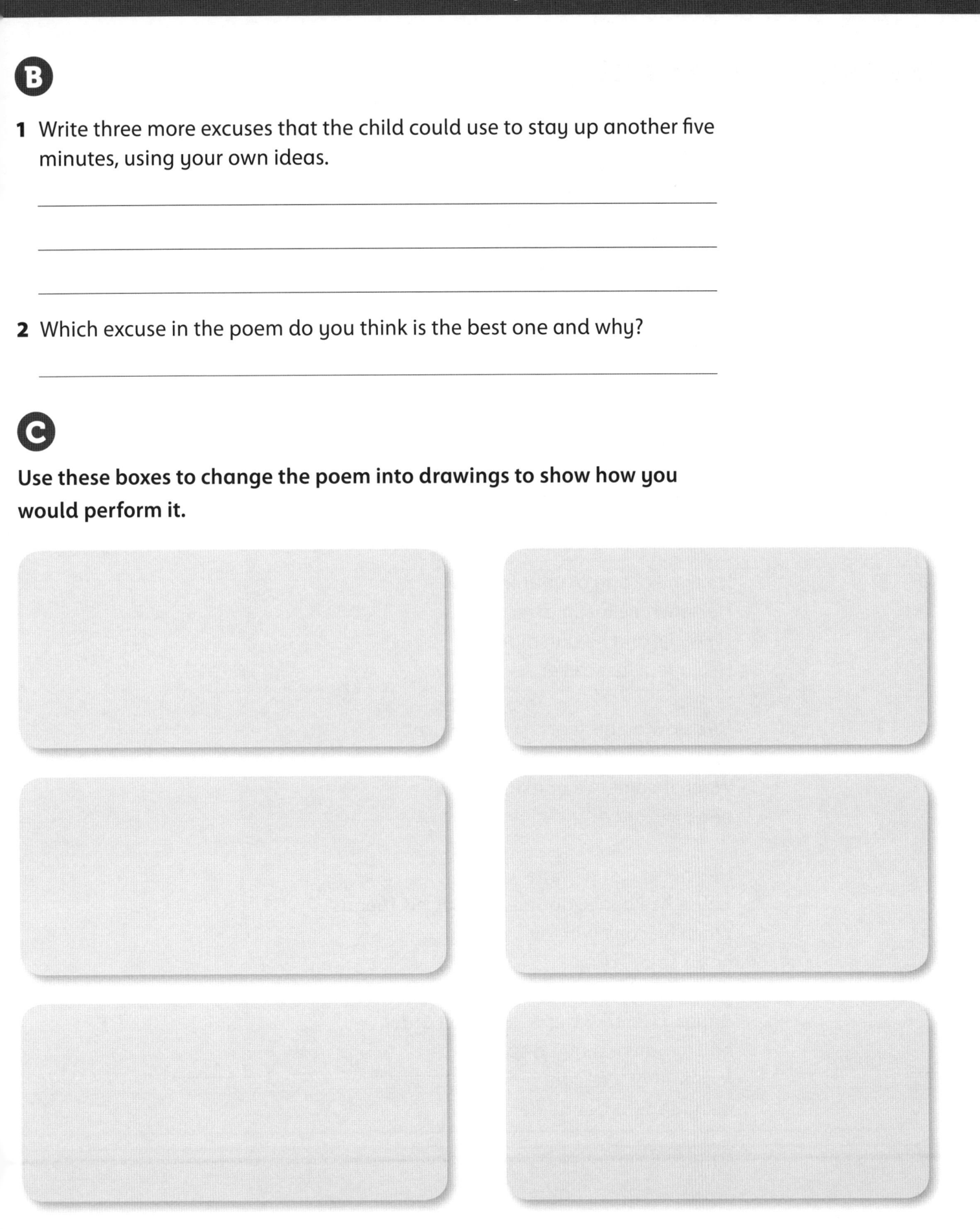

Poetry Reading and writing • Student book page 145

B

1 Write three more excuses that the child could use to stay up another five minutes, using your own ideas.

_____

_____

_____

2 Which excuse in the poem do you think is the best one and why?

_____

C

Use these boxes to change the poem into drawings to show how you would perform it.

Performance poetry

Anancy

Anancy is a trickster of no small order
half a man and half a spider
Miss Muffet was sure glad
he hadn't sat beside her

He's unlike any of your friends
He's a whole lot smarter
He tricks and he outsmarts
He's a real fast talker

He's slow on his feet
a zip on his wit
When it comes to thinking quick
he's a wizard at tricks

He's never lost a game
'cause he cheats, double-crosses his friends
When he can't win fair
he's a spider again

Anancy is a trickster of no small order
half a man and half a spider
Miss Muffet was sure glad
he hadn't sat beside her

Lillian Allen

Comprehension

A

If you were reading this poem out loud:

1 How fast would you read it?

2 How loud would you read it?

3 Where would you include hand gestures?

4 Which words would you stress in verse 2?

B

1 Sum up the 'story' of the poem in three sentences.

2 Why does the poet keep the first and last verses the same? Choose a, b or c.
   a So they act like a chorus that the reader can remember easily.
   b There is nothing new to say about Anancy.
   c Poems should always have the same beginning and ending.

3 On a separate piece of paper, draw five big boxes. Then draw what happens in each verse in one of the boxes. Together, the boxes should look like a comic strip.

4 Choose one quotation from each verse and write this at the bottom of the box. It should match the drawing.

Silent vowels

A
Circle the silent vowel in the words below.

chocolate

poisonous

evening

jewellery

miniature

B
Underline the correct spelling out of the following pairs of words.

parlament/parliament

environment/enviroment

dictonary/dictionary

temprature/temperature

business/busness

C

1 Name two months of the year that have silent vowels.

_____

2 Name two days of the week that have silent vowels.

_____

Forming plurals

Following spelling patterns

A

Add –s or –es to the following nouns to make them plural.

lunch ____   box ____   cat ____   dish ____   door ____

tomato ____   day ____   watch ____   table ____   wish ____

radio ____   tree ____   glass ____   pear ____   book ____

piano ____   pea ____

B

Make these singular nouns into plurals. Remember the rules. You may need to change the **y**, the **f** or the **fe** before adding **s**.

half _____   fly _____   party _____   story _____   berry _____

tray _____   toy _____   baby _____   calf _____   jelly _____

lady _____   knife _____   curry _____   day _____

C

Some plural nouns do not follow clear rules. What are the plurals of the following nouns?

child _____   foot _____

tooth _____   oasis _____

sheep _____   man _____

woman _____   fish _____

mouse _____   person _____

Poetry Writing • Student book pages 154 and 155

Performance poetry

Performance poems use rhythm and rhyme to keep the audience's attention.

Read the first verse of 'In My Bedroom' below. Then write the rest of the verses, remembering to keep the rhyme and a rhythm going all the way through.

A

In My Bedroom

In my bedroom my cuddly old bear
Is losing all his golden hair.

In my bedroom my story book

Is _____

In my bedroom my ticking clock

Is _____

In my bedroom my _____

Is _____

In my bedroom my _____

Is _____

In my bedroom my _____

Is _____

B

On a separate sheet of paper, write a poem called 'In My Classroom'. Use the structure you used in A.

Poetry Assessment

Self-assessment on my learning

Unit 9 A great performance

Name _____

Date _____

🙂 I understand and can do this well.

😐 I understand but I am not confident.

☹ I don't understand and find this difficult.

Learning objective	🙂	😐	☹
Reading skills			
I can find information in a poem.			
I can work out how to make a poem sound interesting if I read it out loud.			
Writing skills			
I can write verses for a poem that contain rhythm and rhyme.			
Language skills			
I can identify prepositions and know how to use them.			
I can identify silent vowels in words in order to help me spell the words correctly.			
I understand spelling patterns for pluralisation.			

I would like more help with _____

_____

_____

Tchang and the Pearl Dragon

A boy sat on the shore of a deep, blue lake in old China. He had been sitting there with his fishing rod since sunrise but he hadn't caught a single fish. Wearily, he packed away his rod and trudged
5 back to the little cottage where he lived.

Now it so happened that a great, green water dragon was passing by. It was on its way home to a far-off river. The dragon had tiny wings and in its forehead was a huge pearl. The pearl flashed brightly in the sun – so brightly that the boy was dazzled
10 and could not even see the dragon. He thought it was just the sun in his eyes.

The boy looked so unhappy that the dragon felt sorry for him. He decided to follow the boy.

His mother was working in the garden, which was just a patch
15 of dried-up dirt. She came running to greet him. "Well? What did you catch?"

He couldn't meet her eye. "Nothing, mother," he replied miserably.

She slumped down on a log with her face in her hands.
20 "Oh, what are we going to do? This land is dried up and dead. We don't have a thing to eat."

The boy was called Tchang. He and his mother slaved all day, trying to scrape together enough to stay alive. But things were getting worse and worse. There were no longer any fish in the
25 lake and very little grew in the barren soil.

The dragon overheard Tchang talking with his mother. Its heart went out to them. That night, when Tchang's mother was sleeping, the dragon gently touched her brow with the tip of his magic wing.

Next morning, Tchang's mother knew just what to do. "You must go and visit the Great Wizard of the West," she told Tchang. "Ask him why we are so very, very poor when we work so very, very hard."

So Tchang kissed his mother goodbye and set out for the West. He carried only a few scraps of bread wrapped up in a handkerchief.

For forty-nine days Tchang trudged across deserts and over mountains until he came to a dark forest. His bread had run out long ago and he was so tired and hungry, he could hardly walk.

Eventually, he reached a tiny house. In the yard, a lovely young girl was drawing water from a well. "Hello, there!" Tchang called. She smiled at him, but she did not reply.

An old lady appeared at the door of the house. "I see you've met my granddaughter, Ai-li," she called. "Please don't mind that she didn't greet you. Since the day she was born, she hasn't spoken a word. It makes me very sad."

Then she looked closely at Tchang. "You look worn out! Come inside and have a bite to eat."

That evening Tchang sat by the fire. He told the pair that he was on his way to ask the Great Wizard of the West a question.

"Good for you!" cried the old woman. "While you're there, could you ask him why Ai-li can't talk?"

The next day, Tchang set off once again towards the West.

Another forty-nine days passed. The food the old lady gave him soon ran out. Finally, he saw a little hut in the middle of an orchard that was scorched brown by the sun. The land looked so dry and poor, it reminded him of home. An old man appeared in the doorway of the hut. "Boy!" he called. "You look worn out! Come inside and rest."

Later, Tchang told the old man where he was going. "You're a good boy to undertake such a difficult journey," said the old man. "By the way, when you see the Wizard, would you mind asking him why my lemon tree won't bear fruit?"

Tchang agreed, of course.

Next morning, he rose early and set off once more for the West. After yet another forty-nine days he came to a river, fast and deep and wide. His heart sank. There was no way he could cross it.

Suddenly, a great green dragon rose from the water. Even to Tchang, who had never met a dragon before, its tiny wings seemed too small for its body. Set in its forehead was a gorgeous pearl.

Tchang was about to run away, but the dragon called to him. "Don't be frightened! I'm quite harmless. Tell me why you want to cross my river."

Tchang explained that he needed to ask the Great Wizard of the West some important questions.

When the Pearl Dragon heard the questions, it smiled. "You're a good lad, Tchang," it said. "Hop on my back and I'll have you across in a jiffy."

On the far side of the river, Tchang thanked the dragon.

"Think nothing of it!" the dragon replied cheerfully. "That's what I'm here for. Oh, by the way. While you're there, could you please ask the Wizard why I can't fly? Every dragon in China can fly – except me."

Naturally, Tchang said yes. He set off again towards the West with the four questions going around and around in his head.

Forty-nine days later, he came to the golden palace of the Great Wizard of the West. The palace was carved out of a mountain. It took Tchang a whole day to climb the million steps up to the huge door. When he pulled on the bell rope, the mountain shook. Flocks of eagles rose squawking into the air from a thousand golden towers.

The great doors of the palace swung open. Tchang found himself in a mighty hall. It was so high he couldn't see the ceiling for clouds. On a throne at the end of the hall sat the Great Wizard. He glared down at Tchang. "Well?" he bellowed. "What do you want, boy?"

Tchang tried to stop shaking. "I … I have four questions to ask you, sir!"

"HAH!" shouted the Wizard. "Then you may as well go home right now! I will only answer THREE questions. If you ask me four, I won't answer any of them. So there!"

Tchang thought his legs would fold underneath him. What could he do? There was his poor mother's question, then the old woman's question, then the old man's question, and then the Pearl Dragon's question. For his own sake, as well as his mother's, he desperately wanted to know the answer to the first question – but he also knew he couldn't let his friends down. So he answered sadly, "Then I will only ask you three."

When Tchang had asked his questions a thunderstorm began to rage high up in the hall. The Wizard hurled three scrolls down to Tchang. "Here are your answers, boy. Now go home!"

Tchang fled from the palace. He leaped down the million stone steps, five at a time.

When he reached the river, the Pearl Dragon was waiting for him. "Well?" it said. "What did the Wizard say?"

Tchang opened the scroll marked 'Dragon'. "He says, if you do something really kind and generous, you'll be able to fly like other dragons."

"Hmm," said the Dragon. "Well, hop aboard and I'll take you across the river."

At the other side, it reached up and prised the great pearl from its forehead. "This is the only precious thing I possess," it said to Tchang. "I'd like you to take it, but when you get home, you must throw it into the lake."

As the dragon handed the pearl to Tchang, its wings grew and grew until it rose slowly into the air. "Look!" it shouted joyfully, "I can fly!"

It was winter, now, and snow lay thick upon the land. Tchang struggled on towards the East until he reached the old man's hut.

The old man was delighted to see him. "So? What did the Wizard say?"

Tchang opened the scroll marked 'Old Man'. "He says you must look beneath the lemon tree."

Together they dug at the frozen earth around the tree until they came upon nine golden jars. Water poured from them, as clear as crystal. As it sank into the ground, all the trees in the orchard burst into flower.

The old man was so grateful he gave Tchang one of the golden jars.

Tchang travelled on until he reached the little house in the forest. Ai-li was away tending the sheep. The old woman said, "So why can't Ai-li speak?"

Tchang opened the scroll marked 'Old Woman'. He replied, "She will speak when she loves someone with all her heart."

Then the door opened and there stood Ai-li. "Tchang!" she cried.

The old woman was overjoyed. She told Tchang, "You should marry my granddaughter. She will make you a wonderful wife."

So Tchang and Ai-li were married.

Then they set off again towards the East. Eventually, they reached Tchang's home. His mother didn't see them coming – she had cried for so long, she had gone blind.

Tchang's heart was heavy. How would he tell her that he hadn't even asked the Wizard her question? Then he remembered the pearl. As he took it from his pocket, the light from the pearl shone into his mother's eyes and suddenly she could see again.

Remembering what the dragon had told him, Tchang ran to the lake. He threw the pearl into its deep blue waters. The lake seemed to shudder and heave. Then Tchang saw that it was teeming with fine, fat fish that jumped right out of the water onto the shore.

Tchang unpacked the golden jar. The crystal clear water poured out onto the garden and a forest of flowers sprang from the earth.

Their troubles were finally over. Tchang lived with his mother and Ai-li and their children for many long and happy years. And every day, the Pearl Dragon would soar high overhead and smile down upon them.

From *Dragon Tales* by Andy Blackford

Word cloud dictionary

Aa

accompany *verb* to go somewhere with someone
acetate *noun* a transparent sheet of plastic that you can draw on
achievement *noun* something that you succeed in doing
advance *noun* improvement or progress
adventurer *noun* a person who goes on unusual, exciting or dangerous journeys
agog *adjective* excited, anxious
altimeter *noun* an instrument used in aircraft for showing the height above sea level
ancestor *noun* a family member in the past who you are descended from
angry *adjective* feeling anger (a strong feeling that you want to quarrel or fight with someone)
animate *verb* give life to
animated *adjective* (for a film) made by photographing a series of still pictures and showing them rapidly one after another, so they appear to move
animator *noun* a person who animates films
anthology *noun* a collection of poems, stories, or songs in one book
ardour *(US spelling ardor) noun* great enthusiasm or passion
armour *noun* a metal suit to protect you from danger
artwork *noun* photographs and illustrations in books, newspapers and magazines
astronaut *noun* someone who travels in a spacecraft
attribute *noun* a quality or feature
avocado *noun* a tropical fruit with a soft pale green oily flesh, often eaten in salads

Bb

ban *verb* forbid people to do something
bare *adjective* not covered with anything
bellow *verb* roar or shout loudly and deeply
blacken *verb* to make something black
blast off *verb* when a rocket is launched, it blasts off (takes off)
bleary *adjective* bleary eyes are tired and do not see clearly
Blue Planet *noun* planet Earth is called 'blue' because it looks blue from space
bluntly *adverb* directly, not trying to be polite
bold *adjective* brave and adventurous

Word Cloud dictionary

booster *noun* an additional engine or rocket for a spacecraft
brainstorm *verb* suggest ideas and then discuss them
brave *adjective* ready to face danger or suffering
break a story *idiom* write and publish a new important news report
brittle *adjective* easy to break
bronze *noun* a yellow-brown colour, like the metal mixture of copper and tin
bulge *verb* stick out or swell
burner *noun* the part of a hot air balloon that produces a flame
burrow *verb* make a hole or tunnel by digging
by the way *idiom* an expression used as an aside, an extra

Cc

cable *noun* a thick metal wire
cacao *noun* a tropical tree with a seed from which cocoa and chocolate are made
calendar *noun* a year planner
camera *noun* a piece of equipment for taking photographs, films, or television pictures
cannonball *noun* a heavy metal or stone ball fired from a cannon
canopy *noun* the fabric part of the balloon that fills with hot air
career *noun* what a person does to make progress in their life, work or sport
career *verb* move with great speed around a corner or bend
cargo *noun* goods carried in a ship or aircraft
carnivore *noun* an animal that eats meat
cartoon *noun* a series of drawings that tell a story
cascade *verb* fall down like the water in a waterfall
cause *noun* reason, a thing that makes something happen
cavort *verb* jump or dance around excitedly
CE *noun* Common Era
ceramics *noun* the art of making pottery
ceremonial *adjective* to do with a ceremony, or used in a ceremony
championship *noun* a contest or competition in a game or sport
change *noun* the money that you get back if you pay more than the amount that something costs
chilli *noun* the hot-tasting pod of a pepper plant
chore *noun* a routine task, especially in the house
circumnavigate *verb* sail completely round something, such as the world
civilisation *noun* a society or culture with an organised way of life
clay *noun* a sticky kind of earth, used for making bricks and pottery
clever *adjective* quick to learn and understand things

Word Cloud dictionary

cockerel *noun* a male chicken
cockpit *noun* the place in an aircraft where the pilot sits
cockroach *noun* a large dark brown insect with wings
comic strip *noun* a series of drawings that tell a story mostly in pictures
compartment *noun* a section or part of a larger enclosed space
compass *noun* an instrument that shows which direction you are facing
computer generated *adjective* created by computer software
confusion *noun* being puzzled or muddled
consumer *noun* an animal that consumes other animals or plants to survive
contrive *verb* to make something happen
control column *noun* the stick that a pilot moves to control the movement of an aircraft
counter *noun* the long table in a shop where customers are served
country *noun* a part of the world where a particular nation of people lives
croquet *noun* a game played on grass where you hit a wooden ball through hoops
cruise *verb* travel gently at a steady speed
cryptosporidiosis *noun* a common waterborne disease caused by a parasite
culture *noun* all the traditions and customs of a group of people
current affairs *plural noun* news about things happening now
curve *noun* a line or surface that bends round, such as the Earth's surface
customs *noun* the usual way of doing things
cutlass *noun* a short, heavy sword

Dd

defence *noun* protecting yourself from criticism or an attack
democracy *noun* a system of government in which all the people can vote to elect their representatives
determined *adjective* having your mind firmly made up
dodge *verb* avoid someone or something by moving quickly
doublecross *verb* deceive someone who trusts you
drama *noun* writing or performing plays
dreamer *noun* a person who wants something badly that they think may happen

Ee

early-learner *noun* a child beginning to learn to read
easy-going *adjective* happy to accept things without worrying or getting angry

edit *verb* choose parts of a film or soundtrack and put them in the right order
editor *noun* someone who prepares a book, newspaper, or magazine for publishing
election *noun* the process of voting for people, especially for members of parliament
emigrate *verb* leave your own country and go and live in another country
envelope *noun* a covering or wrapper; in a hot air balloon, the bag which contains heated air
equality *noun* being equal
exist *verb* be present, be alive
experiment *noun* a test that is done to study what happens
exploration *noun* travelling into space or around a country to learn about it
external *adjective* on the outside
extinct *adjective* not alive now
extraordinarily *adverb* unusually
extreme *adjective* very great or very strong

Ff

fabric *noun* a thin material or cloth
fairness *noun* treating all people equally and according to the rules and the law
famous *adjective* known to a lot of people
feel blue *idiom* be sad
feline *adjective* cat-like
ferocious *adjective* fierce, like a wild animal
fiend *noun* evil demon
fire *verb* put unglazed pottery or clay into a very hot oven and bake it until it is hard
five-penny *adjective, noun* a UK coin
flagon *noun* a container for drinks
flame *noun* a bright strip of fire
flick *verb* move or hit something with a quick, light movement
flight *noun* the action of flying by an aircraft, rocket or bird
flinch *verb* make a sudden movement because you are frightened or in pain
flock *noun* a group of birds or animals
flutter *noun* a light and flapping movement
fond of *adjective* if you are fond of something or someone, you like them very much
food chain *noun* a series of plants and animals, each of which is eaten as food by the one above in the series

Word Cloud dictionary

foot *noun* a measurement equal to 30.5cm
for his own sake *idiom* for himself
foreign *adjective* belonging to or coming from another country
fossil *noun* hardened remains of a plant or animal
freedom *noun* the right to go where you like and do what you like
frothy *adjective* if a liquid is frothy, it has a mass of tiny bubbles on or in it
frustration *noun* the feeling of annoyance when you cannot do what you want to do
funny *adjective* amusing
furious *adjective* very angry
future *noun* the time that will come

Gg

galactic *adjective* related to a galaxy (a very large group of stars)
gazette *noun* a newspaper
gentle *adjective* kind and quiet, not rough or severe
geography *noun* the science or study of the world and its climate, peoples, and products
geyser *noun* a hot water spring coming from the ground
glide *verb* fly smoothly, especially without the use of an engine
globe *noun* the world
gnarled *adjective* knobbly or twisted
government *noun* the group of people who are in charge of a country and run it
GPS *noun* global positioning system which uses satellites to find the position of a vehicle or a person ('sat nav')
grasp *verb* hold something or someone tightly
gravity *noun* the force that pulls everything towards the Earth
grog *noun* a favourite drink of pirates
grotto *noun* a cavern or cave
guardian *noun* a person who looks after an orphan
gyrate *verb* move or dance in a circular movement

Hh

habitats *noun* the places where animals or plants naturally live or grow
haka *noun* a Maori (New Zealand) ceremonial war dance with chanting
hangar *noun* a large covered space where aircraft are kept
haunting *adjective* staying in your mind
herbivore *noun* an animal that eats only plants
hero *noun* the most important man or boy in a story, film, or play

Word Cloud dictionary

home plate *noun* (in baseball) the place where the person hitting the ball stands and where they must return to after running around all the bases

honesty *noun* being truthful, without stealing, cheating or telling lies

hose *noun* a long flexible tube through which gas or liquid can travel

hostile *adjective* very unfriendly and ready to fight

humanise *verb* give something human characteristics

humanoid robot *noun* a machine which looks like a human

hurtle *verb* move quickly or dangerously

Ii

idea *noun* something that you have thought of

identity *noun* who somebody is

illustrator *noun* a person who produces the illustrations in a book

imagine *verb* form ideas in your mind about things that might happen in the future or might be true

in a jiffy *idiom* very quickly

international *adjective* to do with more than one country

interview *verb* meet with somebody to ask them questions or discuss something

invention *noun* the making of something new that has not existed before

ivory *noun* the hard creamy-white substance that forms elephants' tusks

Jj

jam *verb* when something jams, it becomes stuck and difficult to move

jiffy *noun* a moment

justice *noun* right and fair treatment, for example, as based on the law

Ll

laden *adjective* carrying a heavy load

lament *verb* to express grief or disappointment about something

laptop *noun* a computer small enough to be held and used on your lap

lasso *noun* a rope with a loop at the end, used by cowboys for catching cattle

launch *verb* to make something available for the first time

leech *noun* a small worm that sticks to the skin and sucks out blood

letter *verb* to print or paint letters onto something

liner *noun* a large passenger ship

lively *adjective* cheerful, full of life and energy

Word Cloud dictionary

Mm

magazine *noun* a paper publication which comes out regularly, with articles or stories

manufacture *verb* make things with machines, usually in a factory

marathon *noun* a long-distance running race on roads

marketing assistant *noun* a person who helps to tell people about a product or service

marvellously *adverb* wonderfully

Maya *noun* an ancient Indian civilisation from Central America from about 1000 CE

maze *noun* a confusing network of paths or rivers

memorable *adjective* worth remembering or easily remembered

microphone *noun* a piece of electrical equipment that picks up sound waves for recording them

mission *noun* a particular journey, such as a journey into space

mock *verb* tease or laugh at someone

Mom *noun* American for 'mother'

moment *noun* a very short period of time

monstrosity *noun* big and ugly

monument *noun* a statue placed over a grave to commemorate someone who has died

mothership *noun* the plane from which other spaceships are launched

motion capture *noun* computer software that records the movements of people and things

motion sensor *noun* an instrument that detects movement

mythology *noun* the study of myths, old stories about gods and heroes in ancient times

Nn

nationality *noun* belonging to a particular country

navigate *verb* make sure that an aircraft, ship or vehicle is going in the right direction

newspaper *noun* a daily or weekly publication of large sheets of printed paper folded together, containing news reports and articles

no small order *idiom* not a small amount

nonviolence *noun* a peaceful way of bringing about change

nuclear reactor *noun* an installation that produces electricity through nuclear energy

nylon *noun* a very strong artificial (man-made) material

Word Cloud dictionary

Oo
one's *adjective* belonging to a person
oppression *noun* treating people all the time in a cruel, unkind way
optimistic *adjective* expecting things to turn out well
ornithopter *noun* a flying machine
outsmart *verb* do cleverer things than other people

Pp
page-turner *noun* a book that is so exciting or interesting that you have to keep reading it
passion *noun* a great enthusiasm for something, for example, a sport
passport *noun* an official document that allows you to travel abroad
peace *noun* peace is a time when there is no war or violence
pence *plural noun* pennies (UK coins)
personality *noun* your personality is your nature and character
personify *verb* give something human characteristics
pessimistic *adjective* expecting things to turn out badly
plain *noun* a large area of flat land, usually with no trees
plonk *verb* put something down clumsily or heavily
plough *verb* crash violently into something
poison *verb* to kill or harm someone or something with a substance
pollute *verb* to make a place or thing dirty or impure
port *noun* the left-hand side of a ship or aircraft when you face forward
portray *verb* describe someone or something in a particular way
potter *noun* someone who makes pots, cups, plates or other things made of baked clay
pounding *adjective* making a very loud repeated noise
precious *adjective* very valuable
predator *noun* an animal that kills and eats other animals
predict *verb* say that something will happen in the future
presentation *noun* a formal talk showing or demonstrating something
pretend *verb* behave as if something untrue or imaginary is real
producer *noun* a plant that produces its own food from sunlight
professional *adjective* doing a certain type of work or sport to earn money
promontory *noun* an area of land that sticks out into the sea
propel *verb* move something rapidly forward, for example, a boat or aircraft
prune *verb* trim a tree or bush
publish *verb* to print in order to sell (books, newspapers and so on)
pumpkin *noun* a large round orange-yellow fruit with a thick rind

Rr

rant *verb* to speak or complain about something in a loud and/or angry way
ravenous *adjective* extremely hungry
record *noun* the best performance in a sport
reflective *adjective* sending back light or heat
release *verb* set somebody or something free
remote *adjective* far from anywhere else
renown *adjective* being known by a lot of people
retort *noun* a quick or angry reply
rhetorical question *noun* a figure of speech, a question for which an answer is not expected
rickshaw *noun* a small light two-wheeled carriage pulled by a man, used in Asia to carry passengers
ricochet *verb* bounce off something
roar *verb* make a loud deep sound
rocket *noun* a pointed tube that is pushed into the air by hot gases
roll *verb* move along by turning over and over
rustle *verb* make a gentle sound by moving papers or dry leaves

Ss

sarcastically *adverb* mockingly, by saying the opposite of what you mean
sari *noun* a long length of cloth worn as a dress, especially by Indian women and girls
savour *verb* enjoy the taste or smell of something
scatter *verb* to throw things in all directions
scientific *adjective* to do with science
scold *verb* speak angrily at someone
scorch *verb* travel at a very high speed; turn something red or brown by making it too hot
scramble *verb* move quickly and clumsily
script *noun* the written text of a play or film
sentry *noun* a soldier keeping guard or controlling access to somewhere
separate *verb* move people apart so that they are no longer together
shoot *verb* fire a gun; move very fast
shuttered *adjective* with the shutters closed, with the light shut out
shuttle *noun* a spacecraft that travels repeatedly between the Earth and a space station
shy *adjective* timid and afraid to meet or talk to other people
smart *adjective* clever
So there! *idiom* an expression of firmness

Word Cloud dictionary

solo *adverb* by yourself
sonny *noun* friendly name for a boy
sounding *adjective* producing a sound, especially of a loud and pleasant nature
soundproof *adjective* made so that no sound can get in or out
soundtrack *noun* the recorded sound, including speech and music, in a film
spaceman *noun* a male astronaut
spaceport *noun* an airport for spaceships
sponsor *verb* to promise to give someone money if they do something difficult and give the money to charity
spread *verb* lay something out to its full size
sprint *verb* run or move very fast for a short distance
spur *verb* urge forwards
squawk *verb* when a bird squawks, it makes a loud harsh cry
squeamish *adjective* easily disgusted, for example at the sight of blood
squint *verb* look at something with half-shut eyes
starboard *noun* the right-hand side of a ship or aircraft when you face forward
steal home (or 'steal base') *verb* (in baseball) running to a base or to the home plate before another player from your team hits the ball
storyboard *noun* a series of drawings to show the plot of a film, or action in a film
struggle *noun* a great effort, a fight
survive *verb* continue to live
suspend *verb* hang something below something else
suspicion *noun* a feeling that something is likely
swarm *verb* move around in large numbers, like bees or other insects
swat *verb* hit with the hand or an object
swerve *verb* move suddenly to one side
swift *adjective* quick, fast
swing *verb* to move back and forth
sympathise *verb* feel sorry for someone or understand their feelings
system *noun* a way of doing something, for example, in politics

Tt

tabloid format *noun* with square pages
technical *adjective* to do with technology or the way things work
Think nothing of it! *idiom* Don't worry about it!
throne *noun* a special chair for a king, queen or emperor
throng *verb* when a crowd of people throng a place, for example, a square in a city, they fill it

Word Cloud dictionary

toga *noun* a long loose piece of clothing worn by men in ancient Rome
totter *verb* walk unsteadily or wobble
trail *verb* hang down
trailer *noun* a truck or wheeled container that is pulled by another vehicle
tribe *noun* a group of people who live together and are ruled by a chief
trick *noun* a cunning act or scheme intended to deceive or outwit someone
trickster *noun* a person who plays tricks on others
truth *noun* something that is true (believed to be something that actually exists, or happened)
tsunami *noun* a big wave caused by an earthquake
tumble *verb* fall down clumsily
typhoon *noun* a very strong storm at sea

Vv

velociraptor *noun* a medium-sized, feathered dinosaur. It means 'swift seizer'
violence *noun* the use of force to hurt or kill people
Vishnu *noun* a Hindu god
vow *verb* make a serious promise

Ww

wail *verb* cry out with a long sad cry
weightlessness *noun* being free of the Earth's gravity and without weight, so that you float about
whisk *verb* move something away quickly and suddenly
willow pattern *noun* a traditional blue and white pattern on chinaware telling a story
wingspan *noun* the distance across the wings of an aeroplane
wisdom *noun* being wise (knowing or understanding many things)
witness *verb* watch
wolf (down) *verb* eat something in a very quick and hungry way

Yy

yacht *noun* a sailing boat with a cabin for sleeping

Zz

zest *noun* enthusiasm
zip on his wit *idiom* very fast thinker

My vocabulary list

My vocabulary list

My vocabulary list